Gold-Medal
Crafts for Kids

Includes Projects for Children from Preschool to Sixth Grade:

- **Colorful Projects with a Sports Theme**

- **Awards and Certificates**

- **Bible Memory Verse Coloring Pages**

Compiled by Heather Kempton

Gospel Light

Founder, Dr. Henrietta Mears • **Publisher Emeritus,** William T. Greig • **Publisher, Children's Curriculum and Resources,** Lynnette Pennings, M.A. • **Senior Consulting Publisher,** Dr. Elmer L. Towns • **Managing Editor,** Sheryl Haystead • **Senior Consulting Editor,** Wesley Haystead, M.S.Ed. • **Senior Editor, Biblical and Theological Issues,** Bayard Taylor, M.Div. • **Senior Editor,** Kim Fiano • **Associate Editor,** Heather Kempton • **Contributing Writers,** Carol Eide, Dianne Rowell • **Contributing Editors,** Suzanne Bass, Becky Garcia, Karen McGraw, Christy Weir• **Art Directors,** Lori Hamilton, Samantha A. Hsu, Lenndy McCullough • **Senior Designer,** Carolyn Thomas • **Illustrator,** Chizuko Yasuda

Contents

Section One/Prekindergarten-Kindergarten
Crafts for Young Children 9

Section Two/Grades 1-3
Crafts for Younger Elementary 33

Section Three/Grades 4-6
Crafts for Older Elementary 57

Section Four
Bonus Pages 83

Index of Crafts 120

Introduction

Let the Games Begin!

Kids love being part of a team! Colorful jerseys that show they belong. Practicing side-by-side with a common goal. The electricity in the air that says it's game day. The roar of the crowd as the ball goes into the net, over the wall or through the uprights. Your children can experience that atmosphere with the arts and crafts found in this resource book, *Gold-Medal Crafts for Kids*.

As your children create their own works of art and learn about team sports, they'll discover they can all be members of God's team—people worldwide who love and obey Him. As children create their crafts together, look for times to affirm that God loves them so much that He sent His Son, Jesus, so that they can become members of His team. Talk about the ways God shows His love to us. Give them opportunities to ask questions.

We hope that you and your students will enjoy many fun-filled hours creating these projects from *Gold-Medal Crafts for Kids*.

Personalize It!

Feel free to alter the craft materials and instructions in this book to suit your children's needs. Consider what materials you have on hand, what materials are available in your area and what materials you can afford to purchase. In some cases, you may be able to substitute materials you already have for the suggested craft supplies.

In addition, don't feel confined to the crafts in a particular age-level section. You may want to adapt a craft for younger or older ages by using the simplification or enrichment ideas provided for certain crafts.

Three Keys to Success

How can you make craft time successful and fun for your children? First, encourage creativity in each child! Remember, the process of creating is more important than the final product. Provide a variety of materials with which children may work. Allow children to make choices on their own. Don't insist that children "stay inside the lines."

Second, choose projects that are appropriate for the skill level of your children. Children can become discouraged when a project is too difficult for them. Finding the right projects for your children will increase the likelihood that all will be successful and satisfied with their finished products.

Finally, show an interest in the unique way that each child approaches a project. Affirm the choices he or she has made. Treat each child's final product as a masterpiece!

The comments you give a child today can affect the way he or she views art in the future, so be positive. Remember, being creative is part of being made in the image of God, the ultimate creator!

Craft Symbols

Many of the craft projects in *Gold-Medal Crafts for Kids* are appropriate for more than one age level. Next to the title of certain projects, you'll find the symbol shown below. This symbol tells which projects are suitable or adaptable for all elementary-age children—first through sixth grades. As you select projects, consider the particular children you are working with. Feel free to use your own ideas to make projects simpler or more challenging depending on the needs of your children.

suitable for all ages

In addition, some projects in this book require less preparation than others. The symbol shown below tells which projects require minimal preparation.

minimal
preparation

Be Prepared

If you are planning to use crafts with a child at home, here are some helpful tips:

• Focus on crafts designed for your child's age, but don't ignore projects for older or younger children. Elementary-age children enjoy many of the projects geared for preschool and kindergarten children. And younger children are always interested in doing "big kid" things. Just plan on working along with your child, helping with tasks he or she can't handle alone.

• Start with projects that call for materials you have around the house. Make a list of items you do not have, and plan to gather them in one expedition.

• If certain materials seem too difficult to obtain, a little thought can usually lead to appropriate substitutions. Often the homemade version ends up being an improvement over the original plan.

If you are planning to lead a group of children in doing craft projects, keep these hints in mind:

• Choose projects that allow children to work with a variety of materials.

• Make your project selections far enough in advance to allow time to gather all needed supplies.

• Make a sample of each project to be sure the directions are fully understood and potential problems can be avoided. **You may want to adapt some projects by simplifying procedures or varying the materials.**

• Many items can be acquired as donations from people or businesses if you plan ahead and make your needs known. Many churches distribute lists of needed materials to their congregations. Some items can be brought by the children themselves.

• In making your supply list, distinguish between items that each individual child will need and those that will be shared among a group.

• Keep in mind that some materials may be shared among more than one age level, but this works only if there is good coordination between the groups. It is extremely frustrating to a teacher to expect to have scissors, only to discover that another group is using them. Basic supplies that are used in many projects, such as glue, scissors, markers, etc., should be available in every craft room.

Crafts with a Message

Many projects in *Gold-Medal Crafts for Kids* can easily become crafts with a message. Have children create slogans or poetry as part of their projects; or provide photocopies of an appropriate poem, thought or Bible verse for children to attach to their crafts. Below are some examples of ways to use messages to enhance the craft projects in this book.

COACH'S CORNER

Each craft in this book includes Coach's Corner, a section designed to help you enhance craft times with thought-provoking conversation that is age appropriate. The Coach's Corner for a project may relate to ways to grow as a member of God's team, a Scripture verse or a Bible story. Often Coach's Corner includes interesting facts about sports. If your craft program includes large groups of children, share these conversation suggestions with each helper, who can use them with individuals or small groups.

Helpful Hints

Using Glue with Young Children

Since preschoolers have difficulty using glue bottles effectively, you may want to try one of the following procedures. Purchase glue in large containers (up to one gallon size).

a. Pour small amounts of glue into several shallow containers (such as margarine tubs or the bottoms of soda bottles).

b. Dilute the glue by mixing a little water into each container.

c. Children use paintbrushes to spread glue on their projects.

glue level   swabs

OR

a. Pour a small amount of glue into a plastic margarine tub.

b. Give each child a cotton swab.

c. Children dip cotton swabs into the glue and rub glue on projects.

Cutting with Scissors

When cutting with scissors is required for crafts, remember that some children in your class may be left-handed. It is very difficult for a left-handed person to cut with right-handed scissors. Have available two or three pairs of left-handed scissors. These can be obtained from a school supply center.

If your craft involves cutting fabric, felt or ribbon, have available several pairs of fabric scissors for older children.

Using Acrylic Paints

Acrylic paints are required for several projects. Our suggestions:

• Provide smocks or old shirts for your children to wear, as acrylics may stain clothes.

• Acrylics can be expensive for a large group of children. To make paint go further, squeeze a small amount into a shallow container and add water until mixture has a creamy consistency. Or use house paints thinned with water.

• Fill shallow containers with soapy water. Clean paintbrushes before switching colors and immediately after finishing project.

ACRYLIC PAINT

ACRYLIC PAINT

SonGames VBS Craft Leader's Guide

If you'll be leading crafts at SonGames 2004 Vacation Bible School, *Gold-Medal Crafts for Kids* contains more than enough crafts for each age level. For additional hints about leading a group of children in craft projects, see "Be Prepared" on page 5.

The projects in this book can be done in individual classrooms or in a Craft Center. Here's how a Craft Center works:

• Select projects that will appeal to several age levels. (Sometimes you'll find one project that all children will enjoy making. Other times you'll need to select one project for the younger children and one for the older children.)

• Recruit adults and/or youths to prepare for and run the Craft Center.

• Decorate your center with samples of crafts your kids will be making.

• As classes visit the Craft Center, lead them in making projects, tailoring instructions and conversation to the children's age level.

The Craft Coordinator— A Very Important Person

As Craft Coordinator, you play a key role in determining the quality of your craft program. Here are four crucial steps in achieving success at your task:

1. Plan ahead. Familiarize yourself with each day's craft project and plan any necessary changes.

2. Be well organized (see "SonGames 2004 Countdown Schedule").

3. Secure your supplies in advance. Prepare a bulletin notice listing items you need donated from members of your congregation. Also, people are often happy to help if you personally ask them to donate or purchase specific items.

4. Communicate with everyone involved. People who do not know what to do may not ask for help.

SonGames 2004 Countdown Schedule

16 weeks before:

1. List all staff needs. (Will crafts be led by regular teachers or by special craft leaders? Will students from the Youth Department serve as craft helpers?)
2. Meet with the VBS Director to compile a list of prospective staff.
3. Begin personal contacts to recruit needed staff.

12 weeks before:

1. Select projects from this book and list needed supplies.
2. Determine which items are already on hand and which need to be secured.

8 weeks before:

1. Distribute a bulletin notice listing needed supplies.
2. Begin organizing supplies as they are acquired. Separate inventories for each age group are often helpful, especially in large programs.

6 weeks before:

1. Review staffing needs with the VBS Director and plan involvement in training session.
2. Assign leaders to make a sample of each craft project that they will teach to children.
3. Distribute second notice regarding supplies.

4 weeks before:

1. Participate in training session, showing samples of at least the first-day craft projects.
2. Distribute third notice regarding supplies.
3. Make any needed personal contacts to gather required supplies.

2 weeks before:

1. Purchase any supplies still needed. Adjust supplies as needed.

During VBS:

1. Make sure needed supplies are available for staff.
2. Secure additional supplies as needed.

SonGames 2004 Course Overview and Suggested Crafts

Below is an overview of SonGames 2004 VBS with suggested projects for each age level. Each craft has been selected to reinforce the Bible story, lesson focus or memory verse of the day. All projects are fully described in this book.

SESSION	BIBLE STORY	LESSON FOCUS	BIBLE MEMORY VERSE	SUGGESTED CRAFTS
1 JOIN IN!	**God Picks Paul** Acts 9:1-22	God wants me to be on His team and, through Jesus, offers me His love and forgiveness.	**Early Childhood** "God made us and we are his." (See Psalm 100:3.) **Elementary** "Know that the Lord is God. It is he who made us, and we are his; we are his people." Psalm 100:3	**Early Childhood** Waving Flag **Primary** Little League Locker **Middler** Crumple-Art Sports Ball **Preteen** All-Star Photo Board **Optional for All Ages** Team Visors
2 TEAM UP!	**God's Team Helps Paul** Acts 9:20-30; 11:19-26; 13:1-3	God gives me a team so that we can cheer each other on.	**Early Childhood** "Help each other show love." (See Hebrews 10:24.) **Elementary** "Let us consider how we may spur one another on toward love and good deeds." Hebrews 10:24	**Early Childhood** Sports Pack **Primary** Basket Paul **Middler** God's Team Foam Finger **Preteen** Pom-Pom Sports Fan
3 GET STRONG!	**Paul Stays Strong** Acts 16—18:11	God gives me strength to obey His instructions.	**Early Childhood** "I am quick to obey God's Word." (See Psalm 119:32.) **Elementary** "Strengthen me according to your word. I run in the path of your commands." Psalm 119:28,32	**Early Childhood** Counting Sneaker **Primary** Table-Top Soccer **Middler** Whirling Athletes Yo-Yo **Preteen** Get Strong! Barbell
4 KEEP ON!	**Paul Weathers the Storm** Acts 27	God promises to help me through tough problems.	**Early Childhood** "Do not fear, for I am with you." Isaiah 41:10 **Elementary** "Do not fear, for I am with you; do not be dismayed, for I am your God. I will strengthen you and help you." Isaiah 41:10	**Early Childhood** Paul's Big Storm **Primary** Keep On! Discus **Middler** Free-Throw Toy **Preteen** Sporty Spiral
5 CELEBRATE!	**Paul Reaches His Goal** Acts 28	I can celebrate the good things God gives me as a member of His team.	**Early Childhood** "Thanks be to God!" 1 Corinthians 15:57 **Elementary** "Thanks be to God! He gives us the victory through our Lord Jesus Christ." 1 Corinthians 15:57	**Early Childhood** Salt-Art Fireworks **Primary** God's Team Trading Cards **Middler** Beanbag Game Ball **Preteen** Cereal Box of Champions

Crafts for Young Children

Craft projects for young children are a blend of "I wanna do it myself!" and "I need help!"

Because each project is intended to come out looking like a recognizable something, it usually requires a certain amount of adult assistance—preparing a pattern, doing some cutting, pre-selecting magazine pictures, tying a knot, etc. But always take care to avoid robbing the child of the satisfaction of his or her own unique efforts. The adult's desire to have a nice finished project should not override the child's pleasure in experimenting with color and texture. Avoid the temptation to do the project for the child or to improve on the child's efforts.

Some of these crafts have enrichment and simplification ideas included with them. An enrichment idea provides a way to make the craft more challenging for the older child. A simplification idea helps the younger child complete the craft successfully.

Although most projects in this book allow plenty of leeway for children to be creative, some children may become frustrated with the limitations of a structured craft. This frustration may be a signal that the child needs an opportunity to work with more basic, less structured materials: blank paper and markers, play dough, or precut magazine pictures to make into a collage. In any task a young child undertakes, remember that *the process the child goes through is more important than the finished product.*

Waving Flag (10-15 MINUTES)

Materials

- ℣ ¹/₄-inch (.6-cm) dowels
- ℣ saw
- ℣ craft foam in various colors
- ℣ electrical tape
- ℣ 2-inch (5-cm) die-cut letters (available in craft stores)
- ℣ decorative items (stickers, die-cuts, craft-foam cutouts, large sequins, etc.)

Standard Supplies

- ℣ measuring stick
- ℣ scissors
- ℣ hole punch
- ℣ white glue

Preparation

Saw dowels into one 18-inch (45.5-cm) length for each child. Cut craft foam into one 8x12-inch (20.5x30.5-cm) triangular pennant shape for each child (sketch a). Use hole punch to make two holes on the short edge of each pennant (sketch a). Thread dowels through holes in pennants to make poles, and secure with electrical tape on back side of pennant (sketch b).

COACH'S CORNER Sometimes when sports teams win a big game, they're given triangle-shaped flags called pennants. They can wave them in the air to show that they're glad. I'm glad that God loves and cares for us. Let's wave OUR flags and thank God for His love and care. Lead children to wave their flags and sing a short song to thank God.

Instruct each child in the following procedures:

- Glue die-cut letters onto pennant to spell your name.
- Glue decorative items onto pennant.

Enrichment Idea

Children draw on pennants with glitter-glue pens.

a.

8" (20.5 cm)

holes

12" (30.5 cm)

b.

tape

© 2004 Gospel Light. Permission to photocopy granted. *Gold-Medal Crafts for Kids*

Sports Pack (15-20 MINUTES)

Materials

- 1-inch (2.5-cm) nylon strapping (available in fabric or sporting goods stores)
- sports-themed decorative items (magazine pictures, die-cuts, craft-foam cutouts, stickers, stamps, etc.)

For each child—
- paper grocery bag
- two 9x12-inch (23x30.5-cm) sheets of construction paper

Standard Supplies

- scissors
- measuring stick
- stapler
- colored markers
- glue sticks

Preparation

Cut nylon strapping into two 18-inch (45.5-cm) lengths for each child. Fold down the top 2 inches (5 cm) of each paper bag twice (see sketch). To make handles, staple a nylon strap to each side of bag, using two staples at each attachment point (see sketch).

Instruct each child in the following procedures:

- Write your name on one sheet of construction paper. Then decorate both sheets by gluing on decorative items and coloring with markers.
- Glue a construction-paper sheet to each side of your bag (see sketch).

Enrichment Idea

For a bag closure, staple Velcro strips to the inside top edge of bag.

two staples

2" (5 cm)

COACH'S CORNER Sammy, what will you put in your sports bag? People who play sports use bags to hold the things they need to play the game. What games do you like to play? Who do you like to play with? God gives us friends to play with. We can be glad that God gives us good friends.

Team Up! Basketball Painting

(15-20 MINUTES)

Materials

♟ Basketball Sports Ball Pattern (p. 85)
♟ orange construction paper
♟ tempera paints in various colors

For each child—
♟ 12x18-inch (30.5x45.5-cm) sheet of construction paper

Standard Supplies

♟ newspaper
♟ shallow containers
♟ scissors
♟ glue sticks
♟ foam paintbrushes
♟ soap and water

Preparation

Photocopy onto orange construction paper one copy of basketball pattern for each child, enlarging to 150 percent. Cover work area with newspaper. Pour paints into shallow containers.

Instruct each child in the following procedures:

• Cut out basketball pattern and glue it to sheet of construction paper, near the top (see sketch).
• Use paintbrush to spread paint onto your hand. Press hand onto paper to make a handprint.
• Ask several friends to make handprints on your paper (see sketch).
• Wash hands with soap and water.

Enrichment Ideas

Children write their names below each handprint they make. They use orange or yellow markers to make dots on basketballs for dimples.

COACH'S CORNER Your pictures look like many hands playing basketball. To play basketball, the players on a team help each other make baskets. God is glad when we help each other, too. Our Bible says, *Help each other show love* (see Hebrews 10:24). Casey, who is someone who helps you?

Little Sport's Big Medal (15-20 MINUTES)

Materials
♆ duct tape
♆ ³/₄-inch (1.9-cm) ribbon
♆ felt in various colors
♆ star stickers

Optional—
♆ pinking shears

For each child—
♆ large paper clip
♆ discarded compact disc
♆ large gold foil seal

Standard Supplies
♆ scissors
♆ measuring stick
♆ craft glue

Preparation
Make a hanger by taping paper clip to label side of compact disc (CD) so that just the loop sticks over the edge of the disc (sketch a). Cut ribbon into one 2-foot (.6-m) length for each child. Cut felt into one 5-inch (12.5-cm) circle for each child. (Optional: Use pinking shears to cut felt.)

Instruct each child in the following procedures:
• Glue label side of CD to center of a felt circle (sketch b).
• Stick a gold foil seal on the center of the CD (sketch b). Decorate CD with star stickers.
• Thread ribbon through paper clip. Teacher ties ends of ribbon together in a knot (sketch c).

a.

paper clip

tape

CD

b.

c.

COACH'S CORNER A really good sports player might win a medal as a prize. How do you think players feel when they win medals? (Happy.) When you wear your medals, you can be happy that God loves you and helps you. We can all be happy about that!

Salt-Art Fireworks (15-20 MINUTES)

Materials
♈ salt
♈ sidewalk chalk
♈ several shallow boxes

For each child—
♈ 3-ounce disposable cup
♈ 12x18-inch (30.5x45.5-cm) sheet of black construction paper
♈ drinking straw

Standard Supplies
♈ squeeze bottles of white glue

Preparation
Fill each cup one-third full with salt.

Instruct each child in the following procedures:
- Use a stick of chalk to stir salt in cup until the salt changes color (sketch a).
- Squeeze a coin-sized drop of glue onto construction paper.
- Blow through straw, using air to push glue into a fireworks-burst shape (sketch b).
- Sprinkle colored salt onto paper to cover wet glue. Then pour excess salt into a shallow box. (Optional: With teacher's help, pour salt back into cup to use again or share with a friend.)
- Repeat above procedures, using other colors of chalk, to make several fireworks bursts (sketch c).

Enrichment Idea
For a Bible story craft, provide light-colored paper. To show the bright light at Paul's conversion (Acts 9), children make one salt-art burst coming out of a corner. They draw Paul on a road looking at the light (see Enrichment Idea sketch).

a.

b.

c.

Enrichment Idea

COACH'S CORNER Who has seen big fireworks exploding in the sky? People light fireworks to celebrate special times. We celebrate when we're happy and thankful. Rachel, what is something that makes you happy? We can be happy because God loves us and cares for us. We can thank God for loving and caring for us. Our Bible says, *Thanks be to God!* (1 Corinthians 15:57).

Paul's Basket (15-20 MINUTES)

Materials
- brown craft foam
- tan construction paper
- rope material (twine, yarn or heavy string)

For each child—
- sheet of card stock

Standard Supplies
- scissors
- measuring stick
- glue sticks
- hole punches
- colored markers
- transparent tape

Preparation
Cut craft foam into one 4-inch (10-cm) basket shape for each child (sketch a). Cut construction paper into fifteen 1¾x2½-inch (4.5x6.5-cm) bricks for each child. Cut one 2-inch (5-cm) construction-paper circle for each child. Cut rope material into one 2-foot (.6-m) length for each child.

Instruct each child in the following procedures:
- Glue paper bricks onto card stock in rows (sketch b).
- With teacher's help, punch holes near top and bottom of card stock, thread rope material through both holes (sketch c). Knot ends together in the back.
- Draw Paul's face on paper circle. Tape circle to basket so that Paul is peeking out the top of the basket (sketch d).
- Pull knot in yarn to the bottom hole in the back. Turn craft over to front side. With teacher's help, tape basket to the top of the rope. (This will allow basket to move all the way up and down the wall.)

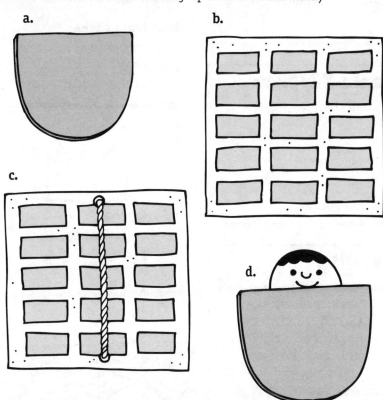

a.

b.

c.

d.

COACH'S CORNER The Bible tells us about a time when a man named Paul needed help. Some people wanted to hurt him. So Paul's friends hid him in a basket and lowered him down a wall with a rope so he could escape. Jaelen, Simon needs a glue stick. What can you do to help him? Claire, what can you do to help your friends clean up? Picking up the paper scraps is a great way to help! Our Bible says, *Help each other show love* (see Hebrews 10:24).

Paul's Big Storm (15-20 MINUTES)

Materials

- Paul Pattern (p. 17)
- white fabric
- brown construction paper

For each child—

- large sheet of dark-blue tissue paper
- 12x18-inch (30.5x45.5-cm) sheet of black construction paper
- wooden coffee stirrer or craft stick

Standard Supplies

- white card stock
- scissors
- ruler
- transparent tape
- glue sticks
- crayons

Preparation

Photocopy onto card stock one Paul Pattern for each child. Cut fabric into one 3x5-inch (7.5x12.5-cm) rectangular sail for each child. Cut brown construction paper into one 7-inch (18-cm) square for each child. Fold each square in half, and then fold in two corners on the folded edge to make a boat shape (sketch a). Tape corners to secure. Cut tissue-paper sheets in half lengthwise.

COACH'S CORNER Paul and his friends were on a ship. There was a big storm with huge waves and strong wind! God kept them safe when they were afraid. Our Bible says, *Do not fear, for I am with you* (Isaiah 41:10). **God keeps us safe, too. He loves us!**

Instruct each child in the following procedures:

- Glue a paper boat a little below the center of black paper (sketch b).
- Glue a fabric sail above your boat (sketch b).
- Glue a coffee stirrer or craft stick onto boat and sail for a mast (sketch b).
- Scrunch one tissue-paper half-sheet like a thick rope. Glue it below your boat to make a stormy sea. Tear second half-sheet into large pieces. Crumple and glue them in the sky for storm clouds (sketch c).
- Color and cut out Paul figure. Place Paul inside boat (sketch c).

Enrichment Idea

Children roll fabric scraps and tie with yarn to make cargo bundles to put in boat.

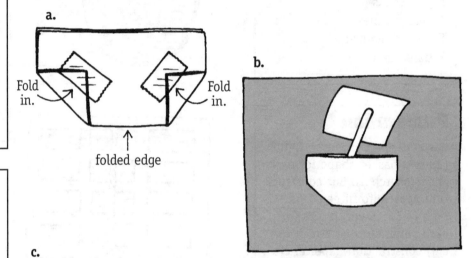

a.

Fold in.   Fold in.

folded edge

b.

c.

16

Paul's Island (15-20 MINUTES)

Materials

- ♈ blue and green crayons
- ♈ twigs
- ♈ red or orange tissue paper

For each child—
- ♈ sheet of sandpaper

Standard Supplies

- ♈ white glue

COACH'S CORNER The Bible tells about a time when Paul was on a ship that sank. God helped Paul swim to an island. The kind people on the island made a campfire to keep him warm. Later, they even gave him food and clothing so that he could go on another sailing ship. God protected Paul. Paul was thankful that God took such good care of him.

Instruct each child in the following procedures:

- Color one edge of sandpaper sheet to be the ocean.
- Break twigs into smaller pieces. Glue twig pieces to sandpaper for a campfire.
- Tear off a small piece of tissue paper and crumple it to make a flame. Glue it to the campfire.

Enrichment Ideas

Children tear off corners of sandpaper sheet to make it into a rough island shape. They use glitter-glue pens to add sparkle to the water.

Paul Pattern
(for Paul's Big Storm, p. 16)

17

Sports Tag Necklace (15-20 MINUTES)

Materials

- ♈ Sports Assortment stickers (available from Gospel Light)
- ♈ plastic lacing
- ♈ card stock in various colors
- ♈ colored dot stickers
- ♈ items to string on necklaces (sports-ball beads, pony beads, dry pasta, circle-shaped cereal)

Standard Supplies

- ♈ scissors
- ♈ measuring stick
- ♈ hole punch

Preparation

Cut plastic lacing into one 2-foot (.6-m) length for each child. Tie a knot in one end of each lacing length. Cut card stock into five 1¹/₂x2-inch (4x5-cm) rectangles for each child.

Instruct each child in the following procedures:

- Place a dot sticker near the top of each rectangle. Teacher punches a hole in the center of each dot to make a tag (sketch a).
- Place a sports sticker on each tag (sketch a).
- String tags and other items onto plastic lacing (sketch b).
- Teacher ties ends of lacing together to make a necklace.

a.

hole   dot sticker

b.

COACH'S CORNER Our Bible says, *I am quick to obey God's Word* (see Psalm 119:32). **God's Word is the Bible. Helping others is one way to obey God's Word. Andrew, Hannah can't reach the stickers. How can you help her? Thank you for giving Hannah the stickers. You know how to obey God's Word and help others.**

Helpful Teammate (15-20 MINUTES)

Materials

- ♆ Teammate Patterns
- ♆ ½-inch (1.3-cm) self-adhesive magnetic tape

For each child—
- ♆ one wooden clothespin (spring-type)

Standard Supplies

- ♆ white card stock
- ♆ scissors
- ♆ ruler
- ♆ crayons
- ♆ craft glue

Preparation

Photocopy onto white card stock one boy or girl Teammate Pattern for each child. Cut magnetic tape into one 3-inch (7.5-cm) length for each child.

Instruct each child in the following procedures:

- Color and cut out your Teammate Pattern.
- Stick magnet to one side of clothespin (sketch a).
- Glue teammate cutout to other side of clothespin (sketch a).
- At home, keep your Helpful Teammate on your refrigerator. Use the clothespin to hold a special paper or photo (sketch b).

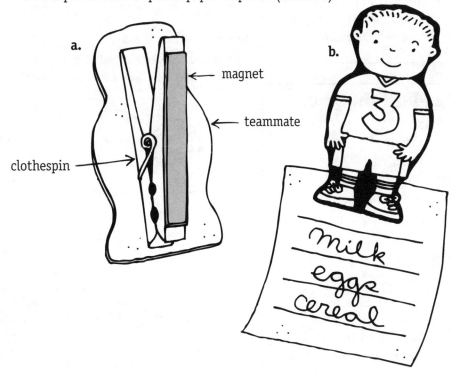

Teammate Patterns

COACH'S CORNER Your Helpful Teammate can hold a note to help your family remember something important. Helping your family is one way to obey God. Tanya, what is something you do to help your family? When Tanya (picks up her toys), she is obeying God. Our Bible says, *I am quick to obey God's Word* (see Psalm 119:32).

Counting Sneaker (15-20 MINUTES)

Materials
- Sneaker Pattern
- yarn
- sports stickers or stamps

For each child—
- 12x18-inch (30.5x45.5-cm) sheet of construction paper
- five hole reinforcements

Standard Supplies
- scissors
- hole punch
- measuring stick
- transparent tape
- markers or crayons

Preparation
Use a photocopier to enlarge Sneaker Pattern as large as possible onto construction-paper sheets. Make one copy for each child, and cut out. Place a hole reinforcement on each lacing eyelet on patterns. Punch a hole in the center of each hole reinforcement. Cut yarn into one 18-inch (45.5-cm) length for each child. Tie a bow near one end of each yarn length; wrap tip of other end of yarn with tape (sketch a).

COACH'S CORNER
Jonathan, how many stickers will you put in this space? That's right! You've done a good job of following the directions. Following directions helps you to finish your craft. God has directions for us in the Bible. His directions aren't about crafts! They're about loving other people. We can show our love for God when we follow His directions.

Instruct each child in the following procedures:
- On the sneaker, place one sticker or stamp in space 1. Place the correct number of stickers or stamps in each of spaces 2 through 6 (sketch b).
- Thread yarn through top hole of sneaker and pull it all the way to the bow (sketch b). Lace yarn through the rest of the holes (sketch c). Tape end of yarn to back side of sneaker.
- Use markers or crayons to color details on sneaker.

Simplification Ideas
Use real shoelaces instead of yarn. Or to make craft into a placemat, omit shoelace and laminate finished sneaker.

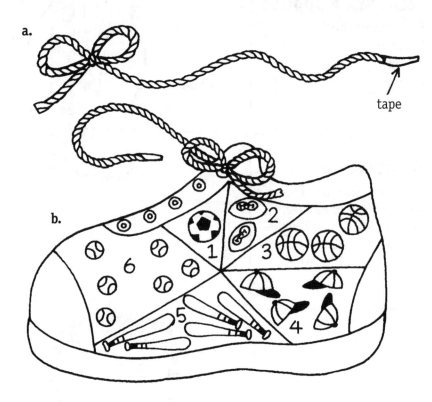

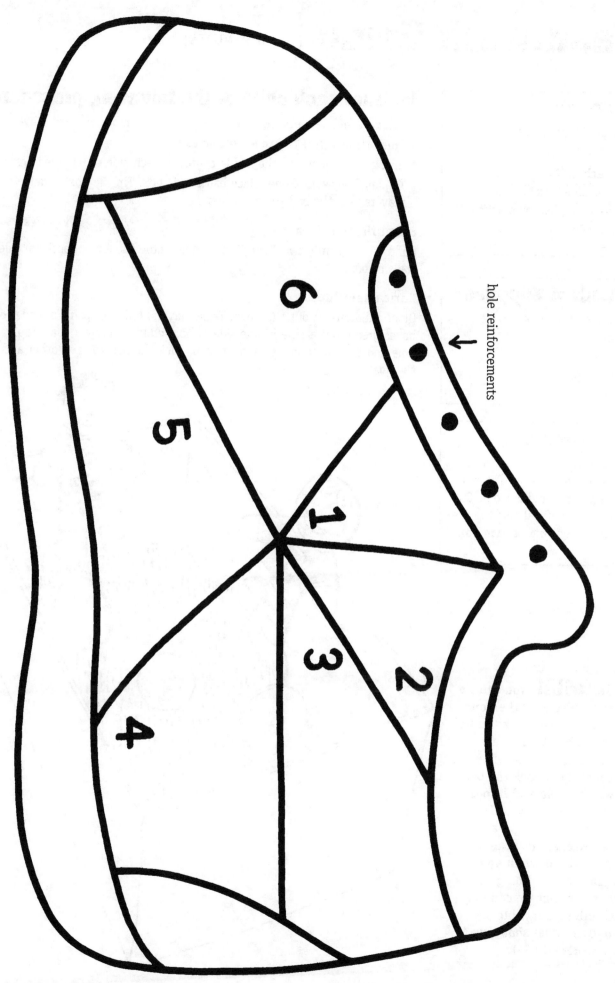

hole reinforcements

Sneaker Pattern

21

Teamwork Game (15-20 MINUTES)

Materials
♈ Team Player Pattern
♈ artificial turf

For each child—
♈ large shoe box
♈ Ping-Pong ball or practice golf ball

Standard Supplies
♈ white card stock
♈ scissors
♈ crayons
♈ white glue

Preparation
Photocopy onto card stock four copies of Team Player Pattern for each child and cut out. Cut a piece of artificial turf to cover the inside bottom of each box.

Instruct each child in the following procedures:
• Color all four Team Players. Write a different number on each player's shirt.
• Glue artificial turf to inside bottom of box.
• Glue a team player to the inside center of each side of box (see sketch).
• To play Teamwork Game, place ball inside box. Tip the box to help the players kick the ball to each other.

Simplification Idea
Children color only two Team Players. They glue them to opposite inside walls of box.

Enrichment Ideas
Older children cut out their own Team Players. Children paint outsides of boxes green. Cut a hole in one side of box; children draw a goal around the hole and tip box to make soccer players kick the ball to each other and into the goal.

COACH'S CORNER You can tip your box to make your Team Players kick the ball to each other. In a real soccer game, players work together to kick the ball down the field and into the goal. Soccer is more fun when players help each other. Rachel, how can you help a friend when you're playing soccer? God gives us friends so that we can help each other! Our Bible says, *Help each other show love* (see Hebrews 10:24).

22

© 2004 Gospel Light. Permission to photocopy granted. *Gold-Medal Crafts for Kids*

Pennant Visor (15-20 MINUTES)

Materials

- ♀ Sports Assortment stickers (available from Gospel Light)
- ♀ card stock in various colors
- ♀ craft-foam cutouts (or scrap craft foam cut into simple shapes)

For each child—

- ♀ craft-foam visor (available from Gospel Light)
- ♀ chenille wire

Optional—

- ♀ Visor Pattern
- ♀ craft foam in various colors
- ♀ hole punch
- ♀ ¼-inch (.6-cm) elastic

Standard Supplies

- ♀ scissors
- ♀ ruler
- ♀ craft knife
- ♀ markers
- ♀ craft glue
- ♀ transparent tape

Preparation

Cut card stock into two 2x3-inch (5x7.5-cm) triangular pennant shapes for each child (sketch a). Cut each chenille wire in half. Use craft knife to cut slits on visors as shown in sketch b. (Optional: Use a photocopier to enlarge Visor Pattern to 150 percent. Trace enlarged pattern onto foam and cut out one for each child. Punch holes where indicated on pattern. Use craft knife to cut slits where indicated on pattern. Cut elastic into one 8-inch (20.5-cm) length for each child.)

Instruct each child in the following procedures:

- Choose a visor.
- Decorate visor with foam cutouts and stickers.
- Decorate card-stock pennants with stickers, cutouts and/or markers.
- Tape each pennant to the end of a chenille wire half (sketch c).
- With teacher's help, thread chenille wires through slits on each side of visor, bend end up, and twist to secure (sketch d).
- With teacher's help, slide slits in ends of visor together, adjusting to fit your head. (Optional: If using visor cut from pattern, teacher threads elastic through holes in visor, places visor around child's head and ties elastic for a comfortably snug fit.)

Enrichment Idea

Provide some of the additional decorating materials listed on the Team Visors idea page (page 84).

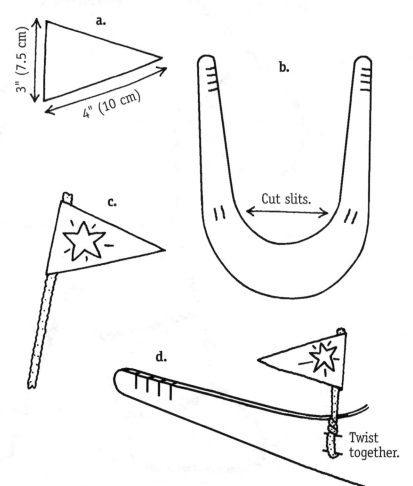

a. 3" (7.5 cm) 4" (10 cm)

b. Cut slits.

c.

d. Twist together.

COACH'S CORNER When their favorite team plays an important game, people sometimes wear funny hats to celebrate. When we celebrate, we show that we are happy and thankful. When are some times that you like to celebrate? (On birthdays and holidays. When good things happen.) People who love God have a special reason to celebrate—God loves us and cares for us! We can thank God for His love and care. Our Bible says, *Thanks be to God!* (1 Corinthians 15:57).

Cut slits.

Punch hole.

Visor Pattern

Punch hole.

Cut slits.

Star-Athlete Picture Frame

(15-20 MINUTES)

Materials

- ♥ Star Athlete Patterns
- ♥ Frame Pattern (p. 28)
- ♥ card stock in various colors
- ♥ self-adhesive magnetic tape
- ♥ decorative stars (stickers, stamps, die-cuts and/or craft-foam cutouts)

Standard Supplies

- ♥ white card stock
- ♥ scissors
- ♥ ruler
- ♥ crayons and/or colored markers
- ♥ glue sticks

Preparation

Photocopy onto white card stock one Star Athlete Pattern for each child. Cut patterns along center lines to separate them. (Hint: Make a few extras, as some patterns will be more popular than others.) Cut out and discard the face opening from each pattern. Photocopy onto colored card stock one Frame Pattern for each child. Cut out frames, discarding the center openings. Cut magnetic tape into one 2-inch (5-cm) length for each child.

COACH'S CORNER Alison, what part of your body can you use to see a baseball? (Eyes.) Michael, what part of your body can you use to kick a soccer ball? (Feet. Legs.) God made your eyes and feet! Emma, what are you using to hold the marker? God made our bodies because He loves us! Our Bible says, *God made us and we are his* (see Psalm 100:3).

Instruct each child in the following procedures:

- Choose a Star Athlete Pattern. Color it to look like you.
- Glue Star Athlete Pattern onto center of frame, lining up face opening with opening in frame (sketch a).
- Write your name on top or bottom of frame. Decorate frame with stars and crayons and/or markers (sketch b).
- With teacher's help, peel the paper backing from your magnetic tape. Stick it to the back of frame, near the top.
- At home, ask an adult to tape a photograph of you to back of craft so that your face shows through opening in frame.

Enrichment Idea

Before class, use a digital camera to photograph the children; print photos so that children can complete their Star Athletes' faces in class.

a.

frame

Star Athlete Pattern

b.

Star Athlete Patterns

Cut out.

Cut out.

Cut out.

Cut out.

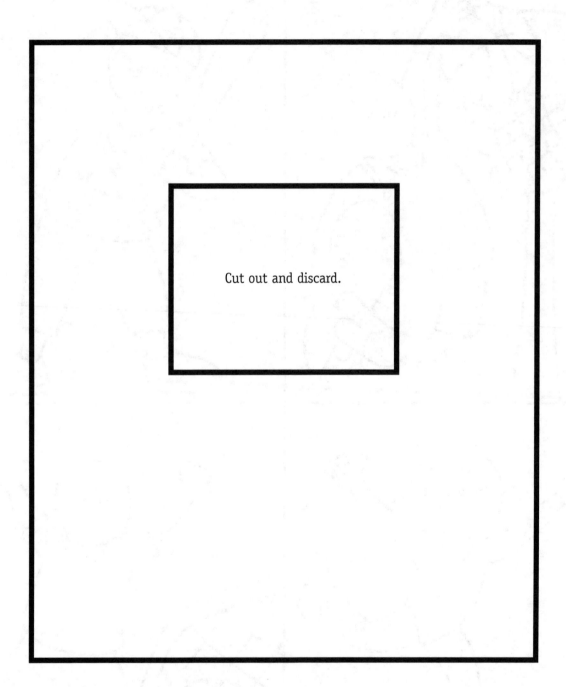

Cut out and discard.

Coach Puppet (15-20 MINUTES)

Materials

♈ Coach Puppet Patterns (pp. 30-31)
♈ Sports Assortment Stickers (available from Gospel Light)

For each child—
♈ one paper lunch bag
♈ two large wiggle eyes

Standard Supplies

♈ white card stock
♈ crayons
♈ scissors
♈ glue sticks
♈ craft glue

Preparation

Photocopy onto card stock one copy of Coach Puppet Patterns for each child.

COACH'S CORNER (Kindergartners) learn lots of new things! Morgan, who helped you learn how to tie your shoes? Simon, who taught you how to write your name? In sports, a coach helps players know how to play the game. The Bible helps us know how to show love to others. God is glad when we do what He tells us in the Bible! Our Bible says, *I am quick to obey God's Word* (see Psalm 119:32).

Instruct each child in the following procedures:

• Color and cut out patterns. (Note: Younger children will need help with cutting.)
• With the bag folded, use glue stick to glue coach's head to flap of paper bag. Glue coach's body to front of bag, below the head (see sketch).
• Use craft glue to glue on wiggle eyes.
• Place a sticker on coach's hat.
• To make puppet "talk," slide hand inside paper bag and open and close hand in flap of bag.

sticker

paper bag

wiggle eyes

Head Pattern

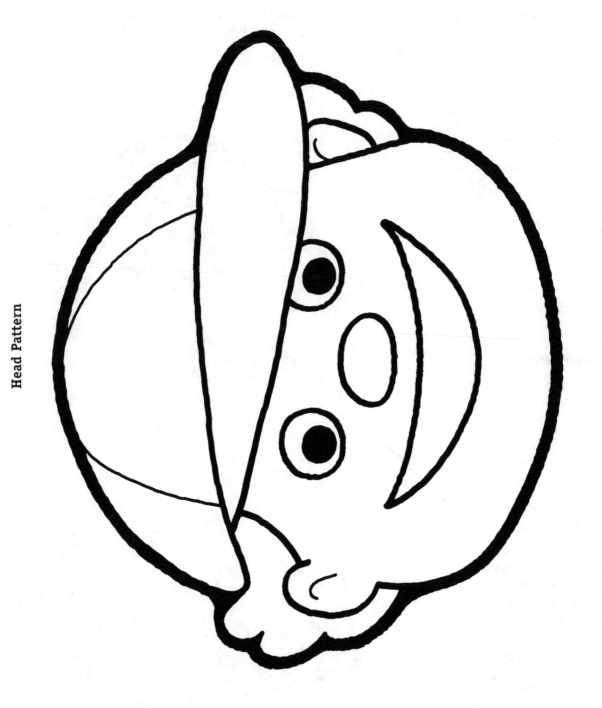

Coach Puppet Patterns

Body Pattern

Crafts for Younger Elementary

Children in the first few years of school delight in completing craft projects. They have a handle on most of the basic skills needed, they are eager to participate, and their taste in art has usually not yet surpassed their ability to produce. In other words, they generally like what they make.

Because reading ability is not a factor in most craft projects, crafts can be a great leveler among children. Some children who are not top achievers in other areas excel here.

You may find additional projects suitable for younger elementary children in the first section of this book, "Crafts for Young Children."

Free-Throw Toy (10-15 MINUTES)

Materials
- string
- black permanent fine-tip markers
- red or orange electrical tape

For each child—
- 9-oz. clear plastic cup
- paint-stirring stick
- practice golf ball (foam or wiffle)

Standard Supplies
- scissors
- measuring stick

Preparation
Cut string into one 2-foot (.6-m) length for each child.

Instruct each child in the following procedures:
- Use marker to draw a net pattern on cup (see sketch).
- Place end of stirring stick against side of cup (see sketch). Ask a friend to hold your cup and stirring stick together. Wrap tape all the way around top of cup and stick for a basket rim (see sketch).
- Attach end of string to ball: For foam balls, tie a knot in end of string and then tape string to ball (see sketch). For wiffle balls, thread string through two adjoining holes and secure with a knot.
- Tie a knot in other end of string and then tape string to free end of stirring stick (see sketch).
- To play with Free-Throw Toy, hold stick in one hand, flip ball up and try to catch it inside basket.

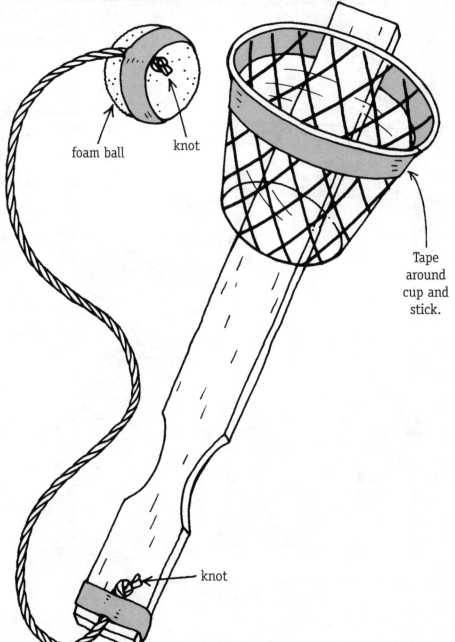

foam ball   knot

Tape around cup and stick.

knot

COACH'S CORNER When you first play with your toy, you might not make a basket on the first try. But what will happen if you keep trying? (You'll get better at it. You'll make more baskets.) **It's good to keep on trying when something is difficult. What other things have you gotten better at because you kept trying? When it's hard to keep on trying, you can ask God for help. God helps people keep going when they are trying to do good!**

Paul's Ship Bookmark (15-20 MINUTES)

Materials

- Ship and Anchor Patterns
- rope material (twine, yarn or heavy cotton string)

Standard Supplies

- scissors
- ruler
- white card stock
- colored markers
- craft glue

Preparation

Cut rope material into one 10-inch (25.5-cm) length for each child. Photocopy onto card stock one set of Ship and Anchor Patterns for each child. (Note: Each child needs two ships and two anchors.)

Instruct each child in the following procedures:

- Cut out all four patterns.
- Color the front side of one Ship Pattern and the back side of the other Ship Pattern. Repeat with the two Anchor Patterns.
- Glue the uncolored sides of the two Ship Patterns together, sandwiching one end of rope material between them.
- Glue the uncolored sides of the two Anchor Patterns together, sandwiching the other end of rope material between them.
- Allow glue to dry before using your bookmark.

Ship and Anchor Patterns

COACH'S CORNER

When Paul was on a ship during a huge storm, the passengers thought they were going to die. But what did Paul say? ("Don't worry. God promised that we'll all live!") **Finally they saw an island! The sailors tossed some anchors overboard and waited for the storm to pass. But the waves tore the ship to pieces! What did the people do next?** (They swam or floated on pieces of the wood.) **Everyone made it safely to the island, just as God had promised! God always keeps His promises.**

Little League Locker (15-20 MINUTES)

Materials

- Padlock Pattern
- craft foam in various colors
- electrical tape
- T-shirt paints or permanent markers

For each child—
- large tissue box
- 1-inch (2.5-cm) metal washer

Standard Supplies

- pencil
- scissors
- craft knife
- craft glue

Preparation

Trace one Padlock Pattern onto craft foam for each child. Cut off and discard the top panel of each tissue box. Trace one small side and one large side of a tissue box onto craft foam and cut out two of each shape for each child. Trace bottom of box onto craft foam and cut out one "door" for each child. Use craft knife to cut vent holes and lock slit in doors as shown in sketch a.

COACH'S CORNER

What kinds of things do athletes put in their lockers? (Uniforms. Athletic shoes. Helmets and pads. Water bottles.) **God's team needs equipment, too! That's why God gives His team things like His love and forgiveness, prayer, the Bible and other Christians to help us grow. God gives His team all the equipment they need!**

Instruct each child in the following procedures:

- Glue craft foam rectangles to all four sides of outside of box.
- Tape the four corner seams where foam pieces meet (sketch b).
- Tape foam door to box (sketch c). (Note: Tape should be on long edge of door opposite the lock slit.)
- Glue a washer to the inside edge of box so that it fits halfway through lock slit (sketch c). Let dry.
- Cut out Padlock Pattern. To close the locker, slide the washer through the slit in the door. Hook the padlock through the hole in the washer (sketch d).
- Use T-shirt paints or permanent markers to write a Bible verse, motto or name on locker door.

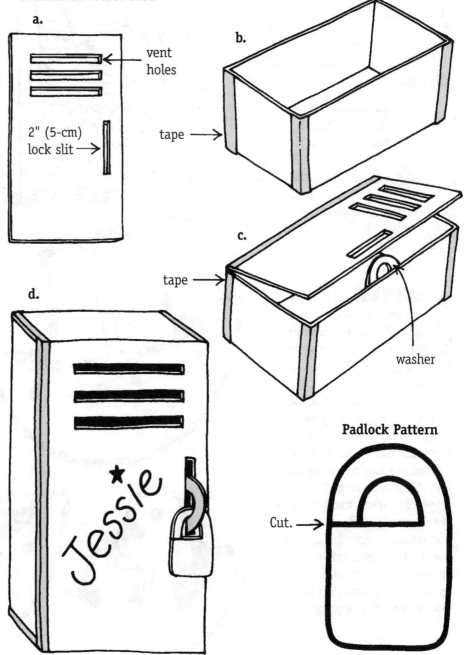

a.

vent holes

2" (5-cm) lock slit

b.

tape

c.

tape

washer

d.

Jessie

Padlock Pattern

Cut.

Celebration Streamer (15-20 MINUTES)

Materials

- 1-inch (2.5-cm) satin ribbon in various colors
- yarn
- metallic curling ribbon
- 3/8-inch (1-cm) dowels
- saw
- electrical tape
- pony beads

Standard Supplies

- scissors
- measuring stick
- stapler

Preparation

Cut satin ribbon into one 5-foot (1.5-m) length for each child. Cut yarn into one 8-inch (20.5-cm) length for each child. Cut curling ribbon into one 3-foot (.9-m) length for each child. Saw dowels into one 18-inch (45.5-cm) length for each child.

COACH'S CORNER Some gymnasts use streamers like this for their routines. They swirl them to make spirals and throw them high in the air and catch them again. It's very exciting! Waving streamers is a fun way to celebrate. You can use your Celebration Streamer to celebrate all the great things God has done for you. The Bible says, *Thanks be to God! He gives us the victory through our Lord Jesus Christ* (1 Corinthians 15:57).

Instruct each child in the following procedures:

- Choose a length of satin ribbon. Fold over about 1 inch (2.5-cm) of one end of ribbon to make a loop. Staple twice to secure loop (sketch a).
- Thread yarn through loop.
- Place ends of yarn together and wrap them with a small piece of tape. Thread taped ends through several pony beads (sketch b).
- Tape both ends of yarn to one end of dowel (sketch b).
- Tape curling ribbon near one end of dowel. Wrap ribbon tightly around dowel to make a spiral pattern. Tape ribbon at the opposite end of dowel to secure. Trim ribbon end.

Simplification Idea

Omit yarn and beads. Children tape satin ribbon directly to dowel.

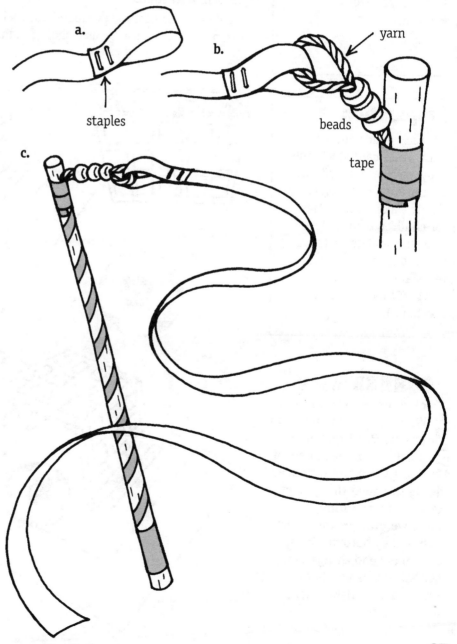

a.

staples

b.

yarn

beads

tape

c.

Table-Top Soccer (15-20 MINUTES)

Materials
♆ Soccer Puppet Patterns
♆ green electrical tape

For every two children—
♆ one plastic berry basket
♆ two sheets of green card stock
♆ two Ping-Pong balls

Standard Supplies
♆ white card stock
♆ scissors
♆ crayons

Preparation
For each child, photocopy onto white card stock one copy each of boy and girl Soccer Puppet Patterns. (Hint: Make a few extras for children who wish to trade boy and girl patterns.) Cut out leg holes of patterns along dashed lines. Cut berry baskets in half (sketch a).

COACH'S CORNER Who has been on a soccer team? What did your team do to practice? All teams need practice! The members of God's team can practice doing the good things God tells us in the Bible. The more we practice them, the easier they become! What are some good things that the Bible tells you to do? (Obey parents. Help others. Tell the truth.)

Instruct each child in the following procedures:
• Tape cut edges of berry basket to one long edge of green card stock for a soccer goal (sketch b).
• Draw a goalie box around the goal on card stock (sketch b).
• Color and cut out both soccer puppets.
• Use crayons to draw large spots on Ping-Pong ball to look like a soccer ball (sketch c).
• To play, place fingers through holes in puppet for legs. Use fingers to kick soccer ball into goal.

Simplification Idea
Instead of coloring ball, children use small stickers to decorate it.

Enrichment Ideas
Children make additional puppets for their soccer team. Two or three children can place their soccer goals a short distance apart for a soccer game.

a.

b.

tape

tape

c.

Draw goalie box.

Fan's Flag Fan (15-20 MINUTES)

Materials
- foam board
- pictures of various national flags
- small objects for children to trace (stencils, cookie cutters, small drinking cups, etc.)

For each child—
- tongue depressor

Standard Supplies
- craft knife
- rulers
- blank paper
- pencils
- colored markers
- craft glue

Preparation
Use craft knife to cut foam board into one 5x8-inch (12.5x20.5-cm) rectangle for each child.

Instruct each child in the following procedures:
- On blank paper, design a simple flag. It can be the flag of a real country or your own design of stripes, symbols and/or words. Use flag pictures for ideas.
- Use pencil to sketch design onto foam-board rectangle. Use rulers and tracing objects for help.
- Color design with markers.
- Poke tongue depressor into bottom middle of foam flag for a handle (see sketch). Remove handle, put a dot of glue in hole, and reinsert handle.
- Use your fan to stay cool during the big game—or any time!

Enrichment Ideas
Provide craft foam or construction paper for children to cut and glue onto flags. Provide star stickers or other small stickers for children to add to their flags. Consider making triangular pennants instead of rectangular fans.

COACH'S CORNER Many sports teams have flags that represent their team or the country their team comes from. The colors and symbols on the flags tell something about the team or country. What does your flag tell about you?

40

Springboard Diver (15-20 MINUTES)

Materials
♆ Diver Pattern
♆ 2x4-inch (5x10-cm) lumber
♆ saw
♆ craft foam
♆ permanent markers
♆ duct tape

For each child—
♆ 1-inch (2.5-cm) metal washer
♆ tongue depressor
♆ blue disposable plastic bowl

Standard Supplies
♆ ruler
♆ pencil
♆ scissors
♆ stapler

Preparation
To make one wedge for each child, saw lumber into 2-inch (5-cm) lengths, forming rectangles, and then saw each rectangle in half diagonally (sketch a). Trace Diver Pattern onto craft foam to make one diver for each child.

Instruct each child in the following procedures:
• Cut out Diver Pattern.
• Thread washer onto thin end of Diver Pattern. Wrap end around washer and staple to secure (sketch b).
• Use permanent marker to decorate Diver Pattern to look like a diver. Bend washer forward so that diver stands up (sketch c).
• With teacher's help, securely tape tongue depressor to wooden wedge to form a diving board (sketch d). Wrap tape around wedge at least once.
• Stand diver on tongue depressor. Gently push end of diving board down and release to catapult diver toward plastic bowl "pool." Try to make diver land in pool.

Enrichment Idea
For an outdoor water game, children fill plastic bowls with water.

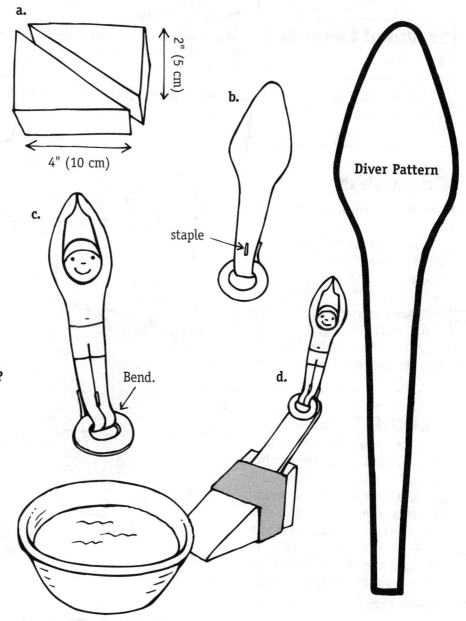

a.

2" (5 cm)

4" (10 cm)

b.

staple

c.

Bend.

d.

Diver Pattern

COACH'S CORNER How many of you have jumped off a diving board? What did it feel like? Divers who compete in events like the Olympics do all kinds of turns and somersaults in the air. How could a good coach help a diver get better? (Teach the diver new dives. Tell the diver how to stay safe. Watch the diver to see what mistakes he or she is making.) In diving, it helps to listen to your coach's instructions! As members of God's team, God is our coach! What are some of God's instructions we can obey?

Team Jersey (20-25 MINUTES)

Materials
- Con-Tact paper
- acrylic or fabric paints
- painting smocks
- discarded children's athletic shoes with high tread (at least one for each color of paint)

For each child—
- child-sized white T-shirt
- sheet of cardboard or a small section of newspaper to fit inside T-shirt

Standard Supplies
- scissors
- newspaper
- shallow containers
- paintbrushes

Preparation
Cut Con-Tact paper to make a large heart, number, cross or fish for each child. (Hint: Make a few extras, as some shapes will be more popular than others.) Place cardboard or a newspaper section inside each T-shirt. Cover work area with newspaper. Pour paints into shallow containers.

COACH'S CORNER Who has worn a uniform? What team or group did your uniform show that you belonged to? People who love and follow Jesus are a team, too—God's team! You don't need a uniform to be on God's team. God loves you so much that He sent His Son, Jesus, so that you can join His team. All you need to do is ask!

Instruct each child in the following procedures:
- Choose a Con-Tact paper shape. With teacher's help, peel paper backing from shape and stick it to the center of your T-shirt (sketch a).
- Put on a smock.
- Use paintbrush to spread paint over the sole of an athletic shoe. Press shoe onto T-shirt to make a shoe print (sketch b).
- Repeat shoe stamping to decorate T-shirt. Place stamps close together, overlapping all edges of Con-Tact paper shape (sketch c). Set aside to dry.
- When T-shirt is dry, remove cardboard or newspaper and peel off Con-Tact paper to reveal a design (sketch d).

Simplification Idea
If you cannot collect enough old shoes, purchase pairs of baby sneakers from a dollar store.

Enrichment Idea
When T-shirts are dry, use iron-on transfer letters, or stencils and paint, to print "God's Team" on backs.

Keep On! Discus (20-25 MINUTES)

Materials

- disposable plastic plates
- tempera paints in various colors
- foam stamps in sports themes or simple shapes (available at craft stores)

For each child—

- two large heavy-duty paper plates

Standard Supplies

- newspaper
- paper towels
- colored markers
- stapler

Preparation

Cover work area with newspaper. Fold several paper towels and place them on each plastic plate. Pour paints over paper towels to make paint pads.

Instruct each child in the following procedures:

- Use markers to print "Keep On!" on rim of bottom of one paper plate.
- Press a stamp onto paint pad and then onto bottom of plate.
- Repeat stamping process to decorate bottom sides of both paper plates.
- Allow a few minutes for plates to dry.
- Staple the rims of plates together to form a discus shape (see sketch).

Simplification Idea

Instead of stamping, children use markers to decorate discuses to look like sports balls or other designs. Provide copies of the Sports Ball Patterns on page 85 for ideas.

Enrichment Idea

To make craft into a rhythm instrument, add a handful of dry beans before stapling plates together.

staple

COACH'S CORNER Your discus is very light. But a real discus weighs as much as six cans of soda (4.4 pounds, or 2 kilograms)! It takes lots of energy to throw something that heavy. Athletes who compete in the decathlon have to throw a discus AND finish nine other events. They RUN in three different races, JUMP in four kinds of jumping events and THROW three different things. No matter how tired they get, they have to KEEP ON going. When we feel tired or discouraged, we can ask God to help us KEEP ON going!

Basket Paul (20-25 MINUTES)

© 2004 Gospel Light. Permission to photocopy granted. *Gold-Medal Crafts for Kids*

Materials

- ♀ Basket Paul Patterns
- ♀ raffia
- ♀ yarn

For each child—
- ♀ two large wooden beads

Standard Supplies

- ♀ white card stock
- ♀ scissors
- ♀ measuring stick
- ♀ masking tape
- ♀ crayons
- ♀ glue sticks
- ♀ hole punches
- ♀ white glue

Preparation

Photocopy onto card stock one set of Basket Paul Patterns for each child. Cut raffia into manageable lengths. Cut yarn into one 4-foot (1.2-m) length for each child. Wrap a small piece of tape around one end of each length of yarn.

COACH'S CORNER The Bible tells about a time Paul was trapped inside a city with a huge wall around it. Some men were waiting outside the gate to kill him! So Paul climbed into a big basket, and his friends tied ropes to the basket and lowered Paul through a hole in the wall, all the way to the ground. You can hang your Basket Paul on your doorknob to remind you of Paul's escape—and to remind you to help other members of God's team, too!

Instruct each child in the following procedures:

- Color and cut out Paul and Basket Patterns.
- Use glue stick to glue basket on top of Paul so that his arms and head stick out the top (sketch a).
- Punch holes in basket and Paul's arms as indicated on patterns.
- Cut raffia into short pieces and use white glue to attach them to basket (sketch a).
- Thread one bead onto yarn. Slide bead all the way to the untaped end of yarn. Knot yarn around bead to secure (sketch b).
- Thread yarn tip down through hole on left side of basket, up through Paul's left arm, down through Paul's right arm and then up through hole in right side of basket (sketch b).
- Thread second bead onto yarn. Cut off masking-tape tip and tie end of yarn around bead to secure.
- Use yarn loop at top of craft to hang craft over a doorknob. Slide Paul to the top of the yarn, and pull yarn ends to make them even. To lower Paul down the door, pull down on each end of yarn alternately (sketch c). To raise him back to the top, gently pull yarn ends apart.

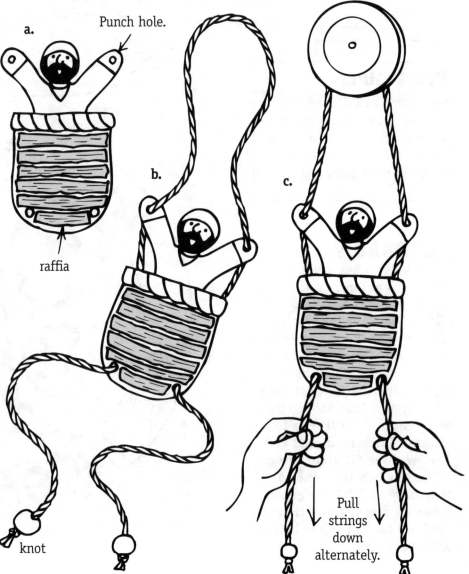

a. Punch hole.

raffia

b.

c.

knot

Pull strings down alternately.

Paul

Basket

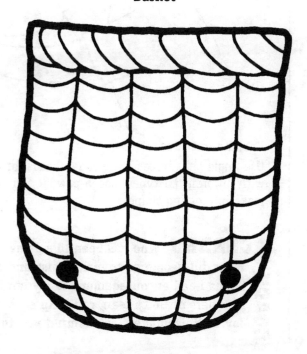

Joyful Noisemaker (20-25 MINUTES)

Materials

- saw
- 3/8-inch (1-cm) dowels
- drill with 1/32-inch (.8-mm), 1/8-inch (.3-cm) and 3/8-inch (1-cm) bits
- 3-mm or thicker nylon cording
- decorative material (colored Mylar shreds, metallic confetti, etc.)
- stickers

For each child—

- clear plastic jar with lid (such as for peanut butter or mayonnaise)
- six large wooden beads
- tack

Standard Supplies

- measuring stick
- scissors
- low-temperature glue gun

Preparation

Remove labels from jars. Saw dowels into one 14-inch (35.5-cm) length for each child. Use 1/32-inch (.8-mm) bit to drill a hole in the center of each jar lid (sketch a). Use 1/8-inch (.3-cm) bit to drill two holes in the side of each jar, directly opposite each other and about 1/3 of the way from the top (sketch b). Use 3/8-inch (1-cm) bit to drill a hole in the bottom center of each jar (sketch b). Cut cording into two 5-inch (12.5-cm) lengths for each child. Plug in glue gun. (Note: Ensure that there is adequate adult supervision for glue gun.)

Instruct each child in the following procedures:

- Tie a knot in one end of a length of cording. From inside jar, thread cording through one hole on side of jar (sketch c). Repeat with second cording length.
- String a bead onto end of each cording length and double-knot to secure (sketch c).
- Push tack through hole in jar lid and then into end of dowel (sketch d). With teacher's help, squeeze a line of hot glue around end of dowel to secure lid. Allow to cool.
- Insert free end of dowel through jar and out hole in bottom of jar for a handle (sketch d).
- Place remaining four beads inside jar. Add a small amount of decorative material.
- Screw lid onto jar, being careful not to dislodge handle. With teacher's help, squeeze a line of hot glue around dowel to secure handle to bottom of jar. Allow to cool.
- Decorate outside of jar with stickers.
- Roll noisemaker's handle between hands to celebrate and make a joyful noise!

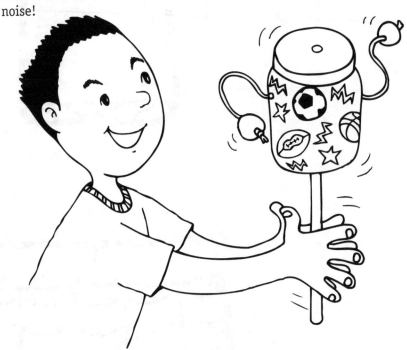

Enrichment Ideas

Use jingle bells instead of wooden beads for a different sound. Experiment with different jar types. Cocoa-powder and powdered-drink-mix containers make interesting shapes.

COACH'S CORNER Who has been to a game with a big crowd of people? What did people do to make noise and cheer for their team? All teams need encouragement to try harder—even God's team! The members of God's team can help each other do their best. Your Joyful Noisemakers can remind you to encourage your friends.

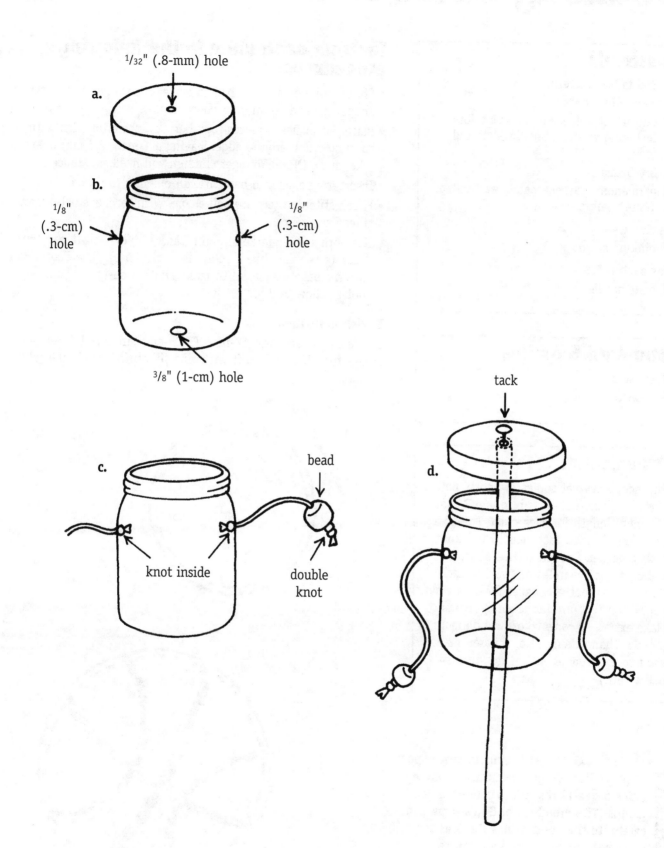

a. $^1/_{32}$" (.8-mm) hole

b. $^1/_8$" (.3-cm) hole $^1/_8$" (.3-cm) hole

$^3/_8$" (1-cm) hole

c. knot inside   bead   double knot

d. tack

Beanbag Game Ball (20-25 MINUTES)

Materials

- Sports Ball Patterns (p. 85)
- embroidery floss
- felt or polar fleece in various colors, including white, orange, yellow and brown
- dry beans
- permanent markers, paint pens and/or T-shirt paints

Optional—
- pinking shears

For each child—
- craft needle

Standard Supplies

- scissors
- measuring stick

Preparation

Photocopy several copies of Sports Ball Patterns page. Cut floss into one 3-foot (36-inch) length for each child. Thread a floss length onto each needle and knot ends together. Cut felt or fleece into two 4-inch (10-cm) circles or two 3x4-inch (7.5x10-cm) football shapes for each child. (Optional: Use pinking shears.) (Hints: Make extras, as some colors will be more popular than others. Also, children may want to experiment with nontraditional ball colors.)

CORNER What is your favorite sport to play? How do you celebrate when you (kick a goal)? It's fun to celebrate good things! The members of God's team can celebrate the good things He does for us. What are some ways we can celebrate and show God that we are thankful? (Sing praise songs. Pray and say "Thank You" to Him. Tell others what God has done for us.)

Instruct each child in the following procedures:

- Choose a kind of sports ball to make. Choose two felt or fleece shapes depending on your chosen sports ball.
- Place felt or fleece pieces together. Sew them together with a running stitch around edge, leaving a 1-inch (2.5-cm) opening (sketch a). (Note: Younger children will need assistance.)
- Insert dry beans into ball through opening to fill ball.
- Finish stitching to close ball shape. With teacher's help, knot thread securely.
- Use permanent markers, paint pens and/or T-shirt paints to decorate beanbag like a sports ball (sketch b). (Use Sports Ball Patterns page for ideas.) Or make another design of your choice. Allow to dry.

Enrichment Idea

Cut felt or fleece into 12-inch (30.5-cm) circles. Children sew circles together and stuff with fiberfill stuffing to make into pillows.

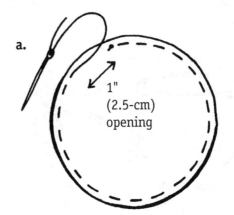

a.

1" (2.5-cm) opening

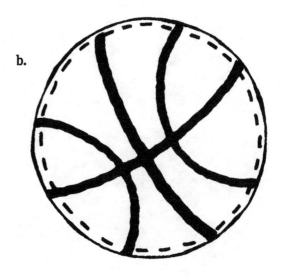

b.

Giant Gold Medal (20-25 MINUTES)

Materials

- ribbon at least 2 inches (5 cm) wide
- spray paint in gold and another metallic color
- small decorative objects (pebbles, twigs, buttons, small leaves, dry pasta and beans, etc.)

For each child—
- heavy-duty paper plate

Standard Supplies

- scissors
- measuring stick
- shallow containers
- craft glue
- stapler

Preparation

Cut ribbon into one 3-foot (.9-m) length for each child. Spray-paint bottom side of each paper plate gold. Spray-paint half of decorative items gold. Spray-paint remaining items another metallic color. When dry, pour decorative items into separate shallow containers.

COACH'S CORNER

CORNER Who has won a medal or a trophy? What was it for? It's fun to win prizes, but they don't last forever! The Bible tells about a prize that WILL last forever—being on God's team. You can't join God's team by running fast or jumping high, or even by being a good person. You can join God's team because He loves you.

Instruct each child in the following procedures:

- Glue decorative items onto gold (back) side of paper plate.
- Teacher staples ends of ribbon to rim of plate for a hanger (see sketch).

Enrichment Idea

Children also decorate medals with glitter-glue pens.

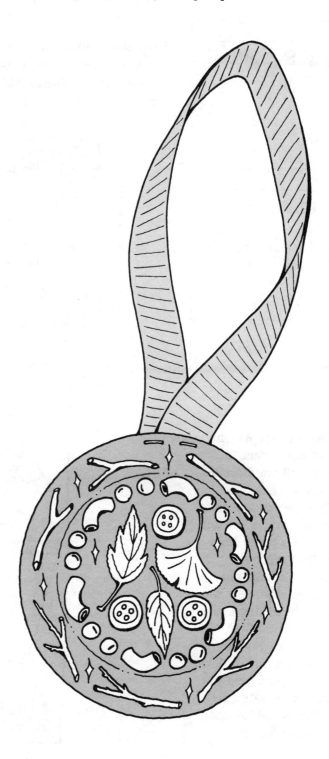

God's Team Trading Cards

(20-25 MINUTES)

Materials

- ♀ Trading Card Patterns (p. 51)
- ♀ Card Pack Pattern (p. 52)

For each child—
- ♀ stick of gum

Standard Supplies

- ♀ white card stock
- ♀ colored markers
- ♀ scissors
- ♀ glue sticks

Preparation

Photocopy onto card stock one copy of Trading Card Patterns and one Card Pack Pattern for each child.

Instruct each child in the following procedures:

- Color and cut apart trading cards. Draw your picture and write your name and age on the MVP card.
- Color and cut out Card Pack Pattern.
- Fold Card Pack Pattern to make a packet for cards. Glue bottom and side tabs closed (sketch a).
- Slide trading cards and a stick of gum into card packet (sketch b).

Enrichment Ideas

Children collect friends' autographs on the back sides of trading cards. They place Awesome Athletes Trading Cards (available from Gospel Light) in their card packs.

a.

glue

COACH'S CORNER People who love God are a team. To "Join In!" all you have to do is believe that Jesus came to save you and then ask God to forgive you and let you be on His team. Then you "Team Up!" with other team members to help and encourage each other. You can "Get Strong!" by asking God to help you obey Him. When something is hard, you can "Keep On!" by trusting in God's promises to love and help you. And you can "Celebrate!" by thanking Him for all the good things He's done for you!

b.

2 TEAM UP!

"Let us consider how we may spur one another on toward love and good deeds." Hebrews 10:24

5 CELEBRATE!

Thanks Be To God!

"Thanks be to God! He gives us the victory through our Lord Jesus Christ." 1 Corinthians 15:57

1 JOIN IN!

"Know that the Lord is God. It is he who made us, and we are his." Psalm 100:3

4 KEEP ON!

"Do not fear, for I am with you. . . . I will strengthen you and help you." Isaiah 41:10

GOD'S TEAM MVP

Name _____

Age _____

3 GET STRONG!

HOLY BIBLE

"Strengthen me according to your word." Psalm 119:28

Card Pack Pattern

Champion Checkers (25-30 MINUTES)

Materials

- Checkerboard Pattern (p. 55)
- Checker Patterns (p. 54)
- one or more toaster ovens and small cookie sheets
- oven mitt

For each child—

- 8x10-inch (20.5x25.5-cm) sheet of unprinted shrink-able plastic (available from www.shrinkydinks.com)
- resealable plastic sandwich bag

Standard Supplies

- white card stock
- scissors
- colored pencils

Preparation

Photocopy onto card stock one copy of Checkerboard Pattern for each child. Using the paper bypass feature, photocopy onto plastic sheets one copy of Checker Patterns for every two children. (Hint: Make a few extras, as some patterns will be more popular than others.) Cut plastic sheets into fourths to separate checkers by type. Preheat toaster oven to 325°F. (Note: Ensure that there is adequate adult supervision for toaster oven.)

Instruct each child in the following procedures:

- Choose two kinds of checkers.
- Color and cut out both sets of checkers. (Hint: All six checkers in a set don't have to look the same, but make sure it is easy to see which checkers belong to which set.)
- Place checkers on a cookie sheet. Teacher places cookie sheet in toaster oven. Bake until cutouts finish shrinking, about one to three minutes. Remove cookie sheet from toaster oven and allow cutouts to cool at least 30 seconds before removing them from cookie sheet.
- Cut out Checkerboard Pattern.
- Play Champion Checkers like regular checkers but with fewer spaces and game pieces.
- Place your checkerboard and checkers inside resealable plastic bag for storage.

Enrichment Ideas

Laminate checkerboards. Children place a small sticker on the back side of each checker so that it can be turned sticker-side up when it becomes "kinged." To make checkers into magnets instead, children stick small adhesive magnets to backs of finished checkers.

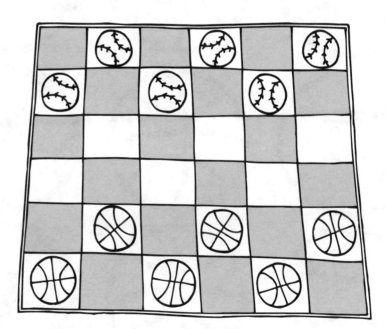

COACH'S CORNER Who has played checkers before? Who taught you? Checkers is simple to learn, but it takes practice to get good! Being on God's team is sometimes like that, too. What are some things God tells His team to do? (Be honest. Obey your parents. Be kind.) It's easy to learn these things, but sometimes it's hard to actually do them! The Bible says that if we ask God for help—and practice doing what He tells us—He will help us get better!

Checker Patterns

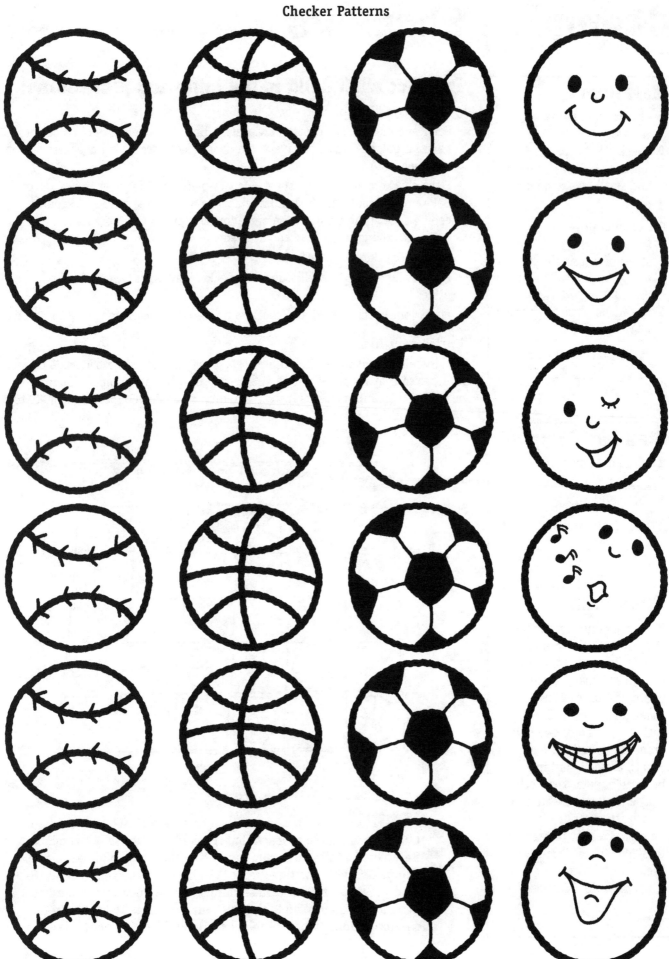

Checkerboard Pattern

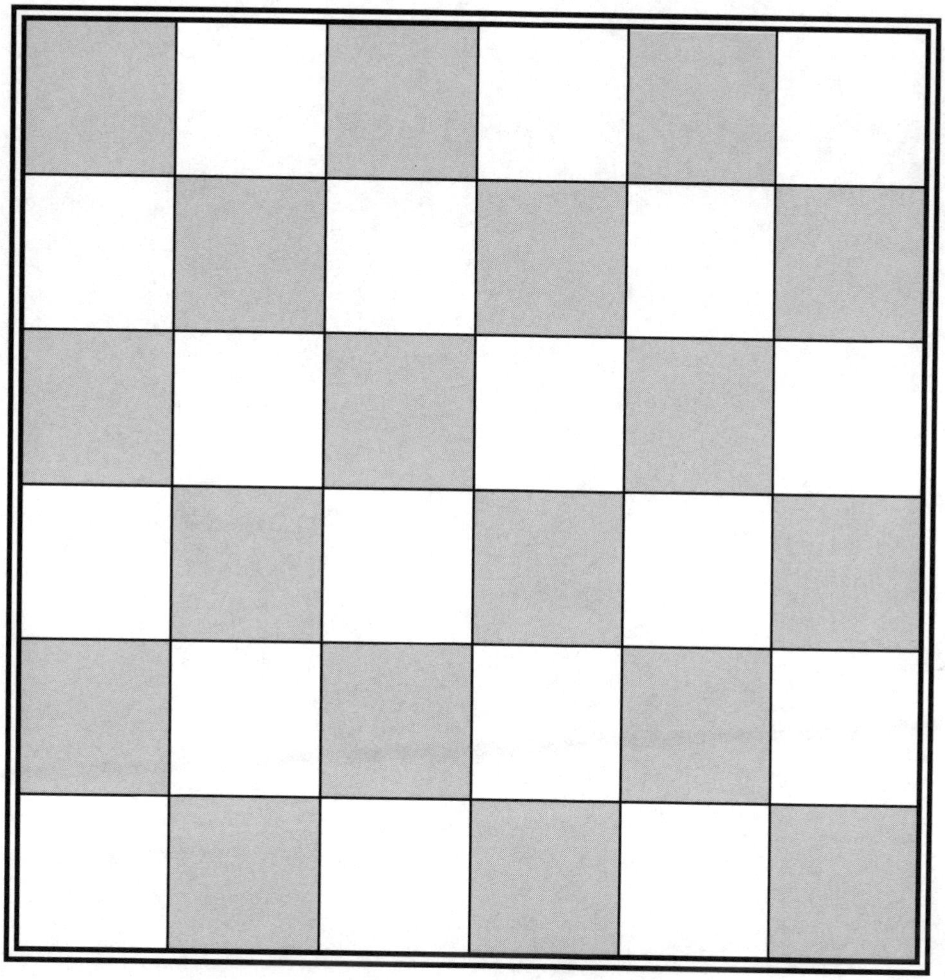

Crafts for Older Elementary

Planning craft projects for older children has driven many teachers prematurely gray. The challenge is that though these children have well-developed skills to complete projects, they also have well-developed preferences about what they want to do. Sometimes a challenging project may not appeal to these young sophisticates, while a project that seems too juvenile to the adult will click with the kids!

We think you'll find projects in this section to satisfy the varied tastes of older elementary children. But a sense of humor and these tips will surely help: Filter craft ideas through a panel of experts—two or three fifth graders. If they like something, chances are the rest of the group will, too. Also, the better you get to know your students, the better your batting average will be. Remember, kids enjoy adapting crafts to express their own personalities—so put out a few extra supplies such as wiggle eyes, glitter glue, and fabric or paper scraps. You just might be surprised at what they dream up!

Whirling Athletes Yo-Yo

(15-20 MINUTES)

Materials

- ❦ Sports Assortment stickers (available from Gospel Light)
- ❦ string
- ❦ small star stickers
- ❦ permanent fine-tip markers

For each child—
- ❦ two discarded compact discs
- ❦ ³/₄-inch (1.9-cm) flat button

Standard Supplies

- ❦ scissors
- ❦ measuring stick
- ❦ low-temperature glue gun

Preparation

Cut string into one 3-foot (.9 m) length for each child. Plug in glue gun. (Note: Ensure that there is adequate adult supervision for glue gun.)

Instruct each child in the following procedures:

- Decorate shiny sides of both compact discs (CDs) with stickers and markers (sketch a).
- With teacher's help, hot-glue button to center of undecorated side of one CD. Apply glue to top of button and press center of undecorated side of the other CD on top, sandwiching button inside CD to form an axle (sketch b).
- Tie a slipknot in each end of string (sketch c).
- Open the slipknot on one end of string and pull loop over CD. Tighten slipknot around button in center of yo-yo's button axle (sketch d).
- To operate, wind string around button axle. Place slipknot at free end of string over finger, release yo-yo, and give it a whirl!

Enrichment Idea

Instead of decorating with stickers, children decorate CDs with acrylic paints or permanent markers to look like sports balls.

COACH'S CORNER Using a yo-yo is easy—once you know how! But learning to do it takes practice. The members of God's team can practice doing the good things God tells us in the Bible. The more we practice them, the easier they become! What are some good things that the Bible tells you to do? (Be kind to others. Be honest. Be thankful.)

Crumple-Art Sports Ball (20-25 MINUTES)

Materials
- ♆ Sports Ball Patterns (p. 85)
- ♆ tissue paper in black, white, orange, red, yellow and brown

Standard Supplies
- ♆ white card stock
- ♆ scissors
- ♆ ruler
- ♆ newspaper
- ♆ white glue
- ♆ shallow containers

Preparation
Photocopy Sports Ball Patterns onto card stock, enlarging to 200 percent. Make an assortment of patterns, at least one for each child. (Hint: Make extras of patterns most likely to be popular among your children.) Cut tissue paper into 2-inch (5-cm) strips. Cover work area with newspaper. Pour glue into shallow containers.

Instruct each child in the following procedures:
- Choose and cut out a sports ball pattern. Choose colors of tissue paper to go with your pattern. (Basketball—orange and black. Baseball—white and red. Soccer ball—black and white. Tennis ball—yellow and white. Volleyball—white and black. Football—brown and white.)
- Tear tissue-paper strips into squares. Crumple each square into a ball.
- Dip tissue ball into glue and press onto pattern (sketch a).
- Repeat to cover entire pattern, using contrasting colors for stitching and lines (sketch b).

Simplification Idea
Enlarge pattern to only 150 percent for a quicker craft.

Enrichment Idea
For a three-dimensional craft, children make two smaller sports balls. They glue them back to back, sandwiching a knotted loop of string between layers for a hanger.

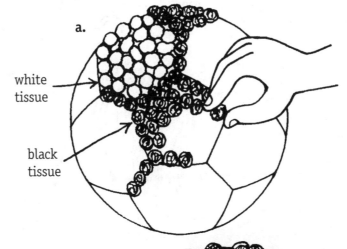

a.

white tissue

black tissue

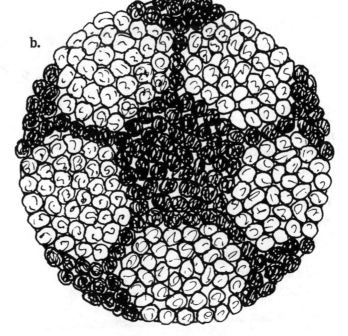

b.

COACH'S CORNER The balls you made represent sports that can be played in teams. But there's a kind of team that is better than any other—God's team of believers! How good must a person be to make a pro sports or Olympic team? (One of the best. Practically perfect.) No one could EVER be good enough to earn a spot on God's team. That's why Jesus came to Earth. Because He took the punishment for our sins, we don't have to make ourselves perfect. We only need to receive God's forgiveness and be ready to join His team!

God's Team Foam Finger

(15-20 MINUTES)

Materials

- ❦ Foam Finger Pattern
- ❦ permanent fine-tip markers
- ❦ craft foam in various colors
- ❦ decorative materials (stickers, sequins, glitter glue, T-shirt paints, etc.)

For each child—
- ❦ paint-stirring stick

Standard Supplies

- ❦ lightweight cardboard
- ❦ scissors
- ❦ craft glue

Preparation

Trace Foam Finger Pattern onto lightweight cardboard and cut out several patterns.

Instruct each child in the following procedures:

- Choose one or two colors of craft foam for your Foam Finger.
- Trace Foam Finger Pattern onto craft foam twice. Cut out.
- Spread craft glue on one side of one foam hand.
- To make a handle, lay paint-stirring stick on top of glue as shown in sketch a.
- Spread glue on top of stirring stick.
- Gently press second foam hand over first foam hand and stirring stick (sketch b).
- Use permanent marker to draw folded fingers and print "God's Team!" or another message on front of Foam Finger.
- Use markers and decorative items to decorate Foam Fingers.

Enrichment Idea

For a giant Foam Finger, enlarge pattern to 200 percent. Omit stick, and glue foam together around side and top edges only, so craft can be worn on hand.

a.   b.

COACH'S CORNER Fans of some sports teams like to hold up giant foam fingers to show that their team is #1! They're encouraging their team to do their best. People who love Jesus are a team, too—God's team! What are some ways the people on God's team can encourage each other?

60

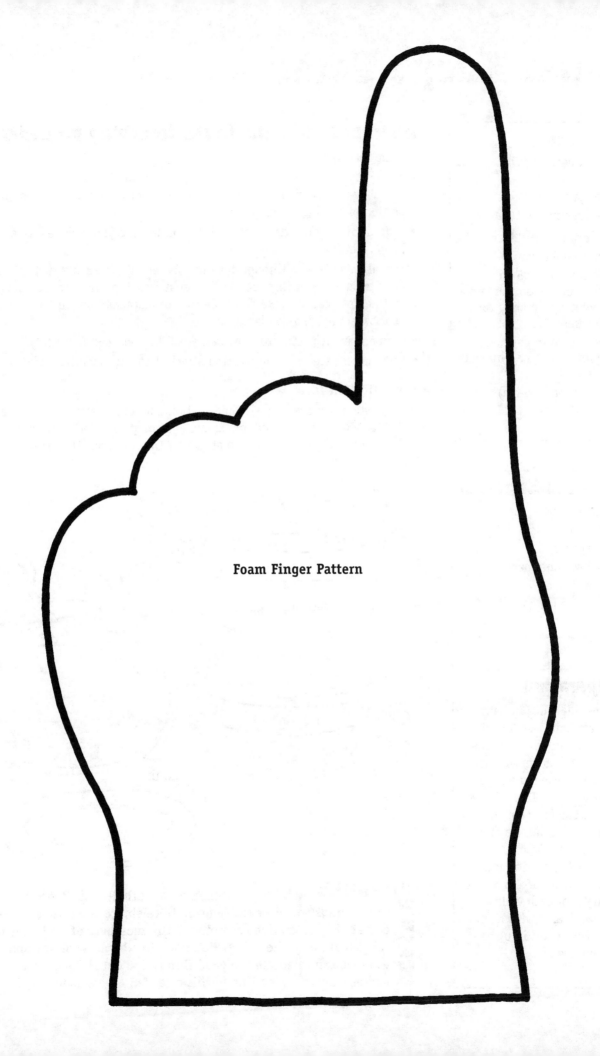

Foam Finger Pattern

Super Hoops Game (20-25 MINUTES)

Materials

- nylon netting (available in fabric stores)
- orange acrylic paint
- black permanent markers

For every two children—
- one chenille wire
- two 5-inch (12.5-cm)-diameter plastic margarine or whipped-topping tubs with lids
- two 2-inch (5-cm) Styrofoam or foam-rubber balls
- two 1-inch (2.5-cm) suction cups

Standard Supplies

- craft knife and/or scissors
- measuring stick
- newspaper
- shallow containers
- paintbrushes
- transparent tape

Preparation

Cut chenille wires in half. Use craft knife and/or scissors to carefully cut off the top 1 inch (2.5 cm) of each plastic tub, leaving an intact ring (sketch a). Discard lower portion. Carefully cut out center of each lid, leaving the outer rim intact (sketch b). Cut nylon netting into one 6x18-inch (15x45.5-cm) rectangle for each child. Cover work area with newspaper. Pour paint into shallow containers.

Instruct each child in the following procedures:

- Paint ball orange.
- Wrap long edge of netting around plastic tub ring, extending 1 inch (2.5 cm) above top of ring (sketch c). Put a piece of tape on the overlapping portion of netting to temporarily secure.
- Snap lid rim over netting to secure to plastic ring and make a basketball hoop (sketch d).
- Thread chenille wire through hole in suction cup. To secure suction cup to hoop, wrap ends of wire around lid rim and ring, pushing them through netting as necessary (sketch e). Be sure to place suction cup on portion of hoop where netting overlaps.
- Use permanent marker to draw basketball lines on ball (sketch f).
- At home, moisten suction cup and attach it to any smooth surface.

Simplification Idea

Omit plastic tubs, chenille wire and suction cup. Cut poster board into 2x18-inch (5x45.5-cm) strips. Children staple ends of strip together to form a hoop and use colored electrical tape to attach netting to hoop. They staple hoop onto card stock to form a backboard.

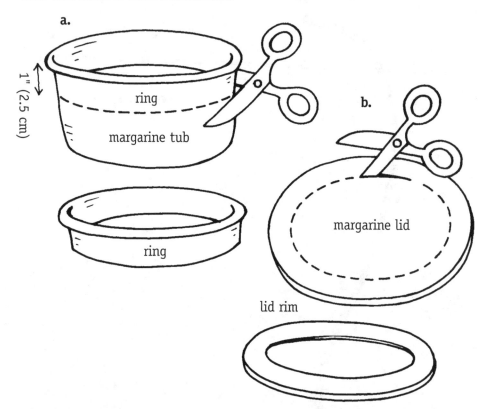

COACH'S CORNER Who has watched a basketball game? What are some things you've seen teams do to celebrate when they win a game? (High five. Hug each other.) **The members of God's team can celebrate all the things He's done for them. What are some ways we can celebrate the good things God does?** (Sing songs of praise. Pray, thanking Him for His care. Tell others about Him.)

c.

ring

tape

overlap

d.

lid rim

e.

Wire suction cup to hoop.

f.

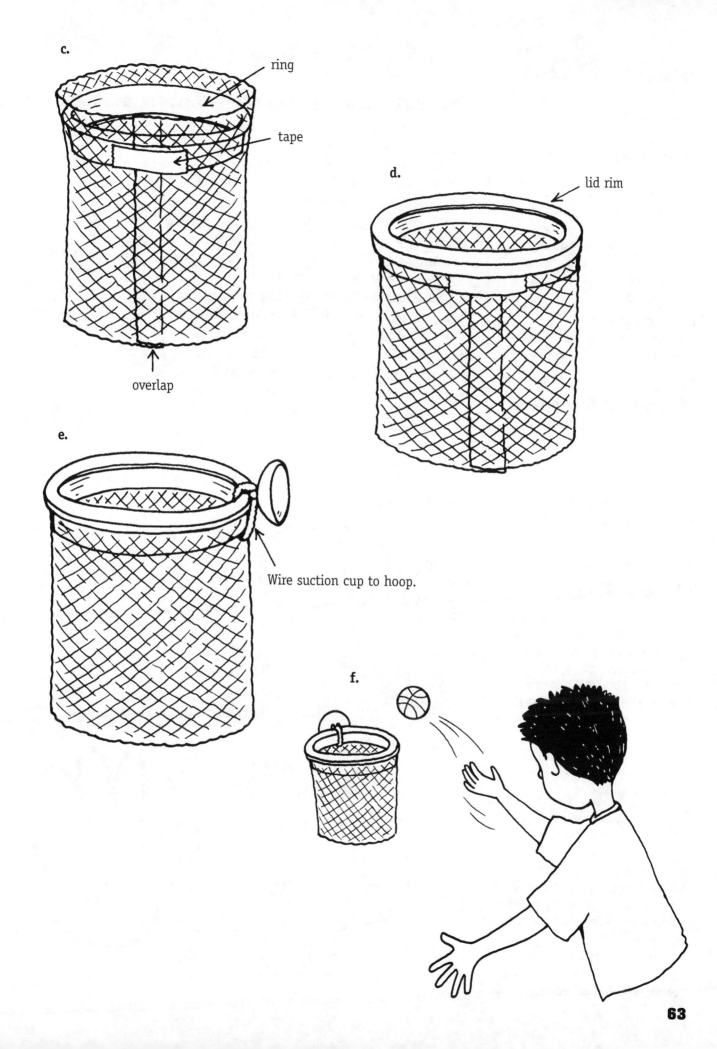

Play Ball! Photo Holder (20-25 MINUTES)

Materials

- Handprint Pattern
- 2x4-inch (5x10-cm) lumber
- saw
- card stock in various colors
- red and black permanent markers
- acrylic paints in various colors, including green, white, orange and yellow
- sandpaper

For each child—

- 18-gauge green floral wire
- 3-inch (7.5-cm) Styrofoam ball

Standard Supplies

- scissors
- ruler
- newspaper
- shallow containers
- foam paintbrushes
- wide-tip markers
- craft glue

Preparation

Saw lumber to make one square block for each child. Trace Handprint Pattern several times onto card stock and cut out to make patterns. Cut floral wire into two 12-inch (30.5-cm) lengths for each child. Cover work surface with newspaper. Pour paints into shallow containers.

COACH'S CORNER

What would happen if a baseball player caught the ball and then refused to throw it to other players on the team? A baseball team that doesn't work together won't win very many games! That's true for members of God's team, too. It's hard to follow God all on your own. That's why God gives us other members of His team to help and encourage us.

Instruct each child in the following procedures:

- Crush Styrofoam ball on table to make a flat bottom side (sketch a).
- Choose a kind of sports ball to make, and paint Styrofoam ball to be the base color of your chosen ball. (Basketball—orange. Baseball, soccer ball or volleyball—white. Tennis ball—yellow.) Or choose your own color.
- Sand rough edges of wood block.
- Paint the top and sides of your wood block green.
- Starting at one end of a length of wire, closely wrap it twice around a wide-tip marker. Slide wire off marker to make photo holder (sketch b). Repeat with the second length of wire.
- Trace Handprint Pattern onto card stock and cut out.
- Use permanent markers to draw lines or stitching on your Styrofoam ball to look like the sports ball of your choice.
- Glue the flat side of the ball to the center of the wood block.
- Insert photo holders into Styrofoam ball (sketch c).
- Insert hand shape into one photo holder (sketch c).
- At home, insert a photograph into the empty wire loop. Write a name or message on the handprint.

Simplification Idea

If children have trouble flattening Styrofoam balls, have them gently rub them on a concrete walkway.

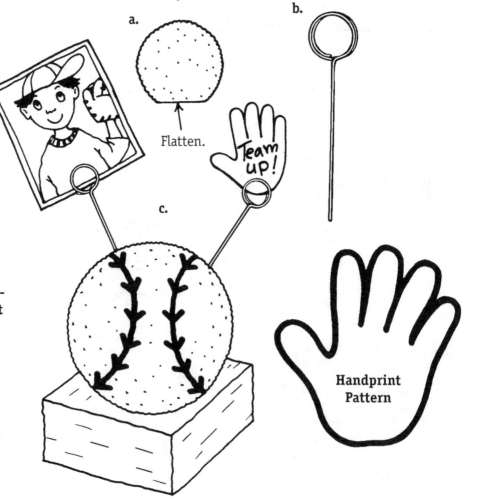

a.

Flatten.

b.

Team Up!

c.

Handprint Pattern

Embossed Gold Medal (20-25 MINUTES)

Materials

- ♈ corrugated cardboard
- ♈ tracing paper
- ♈ gold-colored metal embossing sheets (available in craft stores)
- ♈ 1-inch (2.5-cm) ribbon

For each child—
- ♈ pencil
- ♈ ballpoint pen

Standard Supplies

- ♈ scissors
- ♈ measuring stick
- ♈ white card stock
- ♈ newspaper
- ♈ white glue

Preparation

Cut cardboard into one 3-inch (7.5-cm) circle for each child. Cut card stock into one 2½-inch (6.5-cm) circle for each child. Cut tracing paper into one 3-inch (7.5-cm) square for each child. Cut embossing sheets into one 4-inch (10-cm) square for each child. Cut ribbon into one 2-foot (.6-m) length for each child. Fold newspaper to make one pad for each child, at least ½ inch (1.3 cm) thick and 8 inches (20.5 cm) square.

COACH'S CORNER Who has won a trophy or award? What was it for? People have won prizes for sports victories since before Jesus lived on Earth. But the Bible tells about the best prize we can ever be given—living with God in heaven forever. We don't get that prize because of anything we've done, but because God loves us so much. The Bible says, *Thanks be to God! He gives us the victory through our Lord Jesus Christ* (1 Corinthians 15:57).

Instruct each child in the following procedures:

- Use pencil to trace around cardboard circle onto center of tracing paper (sketch a). Remove cardboard circle.
- Use pencil to draw a design on tracing paper, inside the circle. Keep in mind that tiny details will be difficult to emboss.
- Place newspaper pad on table. Lay metal embossing sheet on newspaper pad, shiny gold side facedown.
- Lay tracing paper facedown onto center of metal sheet. The design should now be backward (sketch b).
- Use pen to trace over design, embossing it onto the metal sheet (sketch b).
- Remove tracing paper. Glue cardboard circle to center of metal sheet. Fold edges of sheet over cardboard circle to secure (sketch c).
- Glue both ends of ribbon to cardboard disk (sketch d).
- Glue card-stock circle over ribbon ends to protect back of medal.
- At home, you can hang your medal from your bedroom mirror or door handle.

Enrichment Idea

Instead of finishing medal with ribbon and card-stock backing, child glues ribbon across the lid of a wooden or papier-mâché box. Child glues back of medal to center of box lid, on top of ribbon (see Enrichment Idea sketch).

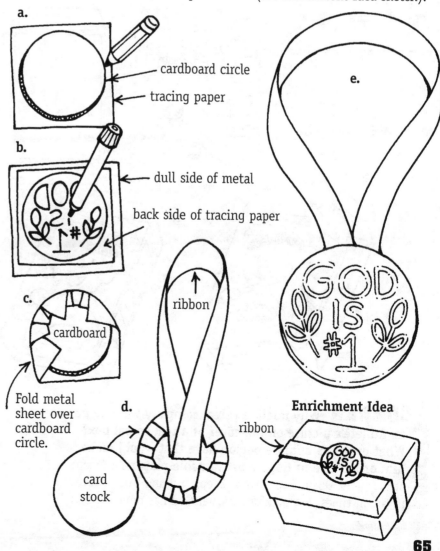

a.

cardboard circle

tracing paper

b.

dull side of metal

back side of tracing paper

c.

cardboard

Fold metal sheet over cardboard circle.

card stock

d.

ribbon

e.

ribbon

Enrichment Idea

Cereal Box of Champions

(20-25 MINUTES)

Materials

♈ Cereal Box Pattern

Standard Supplies

♈ white card stock
♈ scissors
♈ colored fine-tip markers
♈ glue sticks

Preparation

Photocopy onto card stock one copy of Cereal Box Pattern for each child.

Instruct each child in the following procedures:

• Cut out Cereal Box Pattern.
• Draw a picture of yourself on the front panel of pattern (the large panel on the left). Write a name for your cereal on the front of the box (sketch a).
• Decorate the rest of the box any way you choose.
• Fold pattern along dashed lines. Glue "glue tab" section of pattern to back side of "Nutrition Facts" panel (sketch b).
• Fold in all four "side tab" sections. Fold in and glue together large bottom tabs to make box bottom (sketch c).
• Fold in large top tabs to make box top. Box top can be glued for added stability or left open.

Enrichment Ideas

Enlarge pattern onto larger card stock for bigger boxes. Children add a small amount of nonsugary dry cereal to boxes before closing. Have each child bring a photo of him- or herself; child cuts around photo and glues to front of box. Or scan pattern into a computer, take a digital photo of each child, paste photo into the pattern, and use a color printer to print onto card stock.

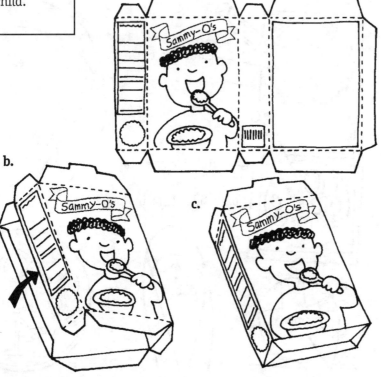

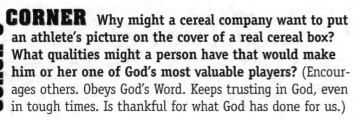

COACH'S CORNER Why might a cereal company want to put an athlete's picture on the cover of a real cereal box? What qualities might a person have that would make him or her one of God's most valuable players? (Encourages others. Obeys God's Word. Keeps trusting in God, even in tough times. Is thankful for what God has done for us.)

Nutrition Facts

Net Weight
1.5 oz. (42)

side tab

side tab

side tab

side tab

glue tab

Cereal Box Pattern

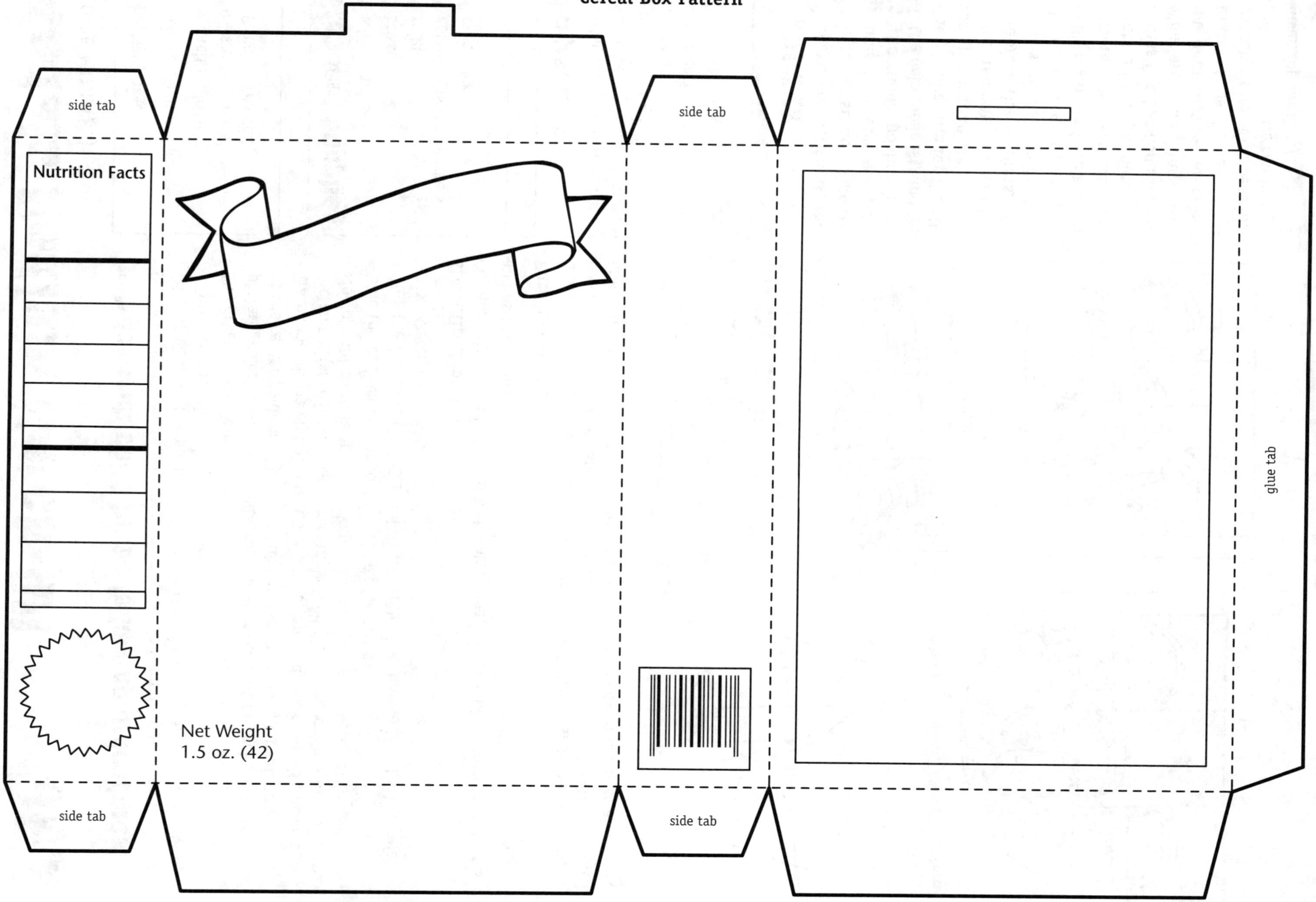

Medals Podium Catch-All

(20-25 MINUTES)

© 2004 Gospel Light. Permission to photocopy granted. *Gold-Medal Crafts for Kids*

Materials

♈ Medals Podium Pattern

For each child—

♈ cereal box, no wider than 9 inches (23 cm)

Standard Supplies

♈ white card stock
♈ scissors
♈ ruler
♈ colored fine-tip markers
♈ glue sticks

Preparation

Photocopy onto card stock two copies of Medals Podium Pattern for each child. Cut off the bottom 3 inches (7.5 cm) of each cereal box and discard rest of box.

COACH'S CORNER At some sports competitions, the winners stand on podiums to receive medals. The middle podium is for the gold medalist, and the side podiums are for the silver and bronze medalists. The ceremony is a way to celebrate the winners, as well as the hard work of all the athletes. As members of God's team, we have a lot to celebrate, too—we can celebrate all the wonderful things God has done for us. What are some things God has done that we can celebrate? (Made the world. Made us. Takes care of us. Sent His Son, Jesus, so we can be forgiven for our sins.)

Instruct each child in the following procedures:

- Cut out only the podium portion of one Medals Podium copy along bold line (sketch a). Color the podiums. Set aside rest of pattern (athletes and crowd) to use as scrap.
- The other Medals Podium copy will be the box backdrop. On top portion of pattern, color the athletes and crowd. On bottom portion, color only top third of the center podium (sketch b). Cut out backdrop along outside line.
- Trace around one end of cereal box onto scrap card stock twice to make two rectangles (sketch c). Cut out rectangles and glue to cover ends of box, blank side of card stock facing out (sketch d).
- Glue the podium cutout to front of box (sketch d).
- Glue the backdrop (athletes and crowd) to back of box so that backdrop faces box (sketch d).

Simplification Idea

Cut out patterns and box-end rectangles ahead of time. Children color patterns and assemble boxes.

Enrichment Ideas

Children cut scrap construction paper into pennant shapes and glue to crowd scene. They glue crepe paper over podium bunting to make it three-dimensional. Children put three small empty vegetable cans inside box to use it as a desk set.

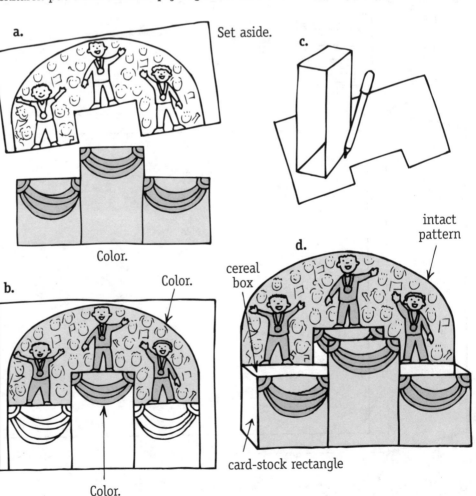

a.   Set aside.   c.

Color.

b.   Color.

Color.

d.

intact pattern

cereal box

card-stock rectangle

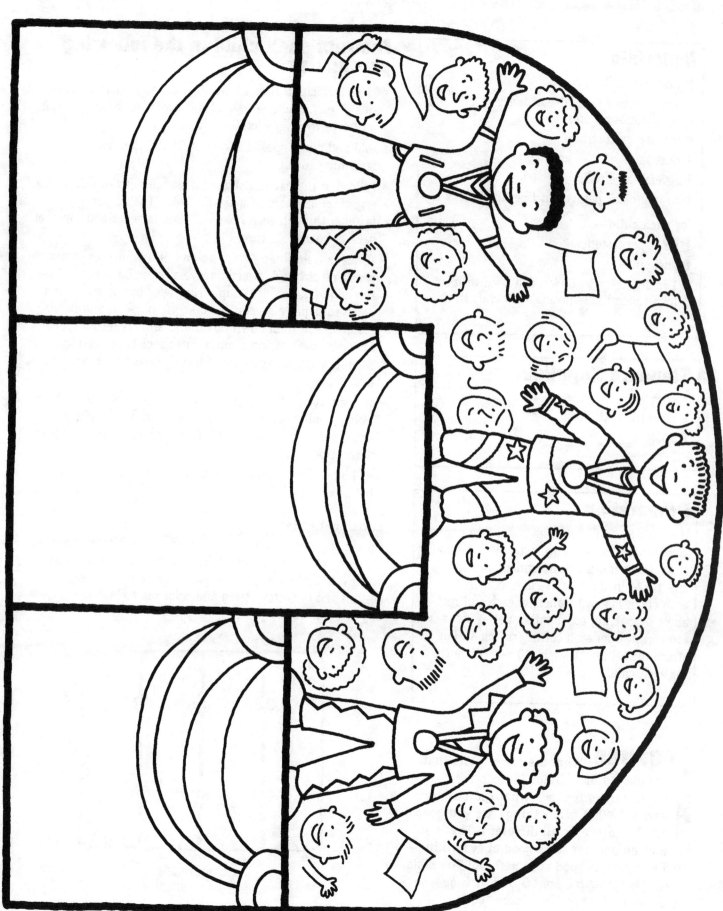

All-Star Photo Board (20-25 MINUTES)

Materials

- foam board
- artificial turf (available at home-improvement stores)
- white cotton string
- duct tape
- several large nails
- several black permanent fine-tip markers

For each child—

- six paper fasteners
- pushpin
- 1-inch (2.5-cm) wooden doll head with 1/4-inch (.6-cm) hole (available at craft stores)

Standard Supplies

- craft knife
- measuring stick
- scissors

Preparation

Use craft knife to cut foam board into one 10x20-inch (25.5x51-cm) rectangle for each child. Use scissors to cut artificial turf into one 14x24-inch (35.5x61-cm) rectangle for each child. Remove corners of each turf rectangle by cutting on the diagonal, 4 inches (10 cm) in from each corner (sketch a). Cut string into three 16-inch (40.5-cm) lengths for each child.

Instruct each child in the following procedures:

- Place artificial turf facedown. Center foam board on back side of turf. Fold one edge of turf over foam board and use duct tape to cover edge (sketch b).
- Fold and tape opposite edge of turf and then two remaining edges.
- Following the pattern shown in sketch c, poke nail all the way through board to make six holes. Push a paper fastener through each hole and bend fastener ends open at back of board to secure.
- To make field lines: Tape one end of a length of string to back side of board, directly above a paper fastener and near the edge (sketch d). Wrap string over top of board and down to paper fastener. Wind string once around paper fastener and then down board and around second paper fastener. Wrap string around bottom of board (sketch e). Tape in place on back side of board. Repeat with remaining two strings.
- To make a sports-ball pin: Glue pushpin head into hole of wooden doll head. Draw large black dots on the pin to look like a soccer ball (sketch e). Stick pin onto the board for decoration.
- At home, slide photographs or small notes under strings to hold them in place.

Enrichment Idea

For a craft with "flower power," children stick paper fasteners through petal portions of artificial flowers before fastening to board (see Enrichment Idea sketch). Children use narrow ribbon instead of cotton string and color pin to look like a ladybug or bumblebee.

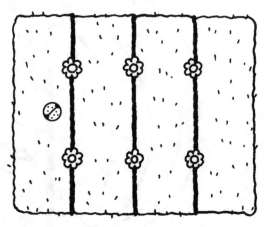

Enrichment Idea

COACH'S CORNER What are some sports that are played on a field? (Soccer. Baseball. Football. Field Hockey.) What sport are you best at? What other things are you good at? God made us all different. That's so that no one has to be good at everything—and everyone is good at something! The Bible says, *Know that the Lord is God. It is he who made us, and we are his* (Psalm 100:3).

a.

4" (10 cm)

4" (10 cm)

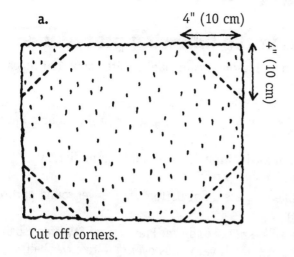

Cut off corners.

b.

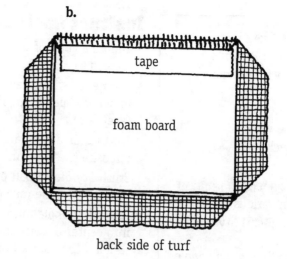

back side of turf

c.

paper fastener

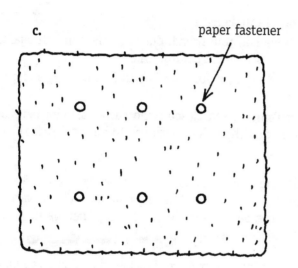

d.

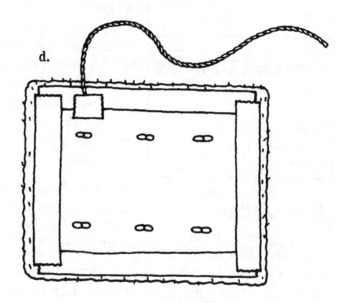

e.

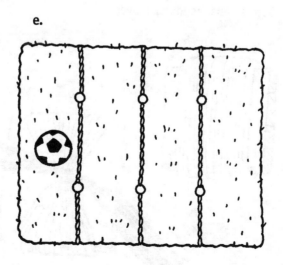

Pom-Pom Sports Fan (25-30 MINUTES)

Materials

- ♆ Sports Fan Patterns
- ♆ card stock in various colors
- ♆ corrugated cardboard
- ♆ chenille wire
- ♆ toothpicks

For each child—

- ♆ about 20 yards (18 m) of yarn in various colors
- ♆ 2-inch (5-cm) Styrofoam ball
- ♆ two medium-sized wiggle eyes

Standard Supplies

- ♆ scissors
- ♆ ruler
- ♆ white glue
- ♆ colored markers

Preparation

Photocopy onto various colors of card stock one set of Sports Fan Patterns for each child. Cut cardboard into one 3-inch (7.5-cm) square for each child. Cut various colors of yarn into six 10-inch (25.5-cm) lengths for each child. Reserve remaining yarn for children's use.

COACH'S CORNER Your Pom-Pom Sports Fans look ready to cheer at the game! Why do people cheer at sports events? God wants the members of His team to cheer each other on, too. Hebrews 10:24 says, *Let us consider how we may spur one another on toward love and good deeds.*

Instruct each child in the following procedures:

- Choose a color of yarn. Wrap yarn around cardboard square about 100 times (sketch a).
- Choose six short pieces of yarn and hold them all together. Slide yarn lengths under wrapped yarn. Tie all six pieces around wrapped yarn in a double knot (sketch b).
- Turn cardboard square over and cut through all wrapped yarn, directly opposite the knot on the other side (sketch c).
- Crush Styrofoam ball on table to make a flat bottom side. Cover round portions of ball with glue (sketch d).
- Lay yarn bundle onto table with knot-side down. Press top of Styrofoam ball into center of yarn bundle and smooth yarn ends over glue to cover ball, forming the Sports Fan's body (sketch e).
- Choose a color of card-stock sneakers and cut out. Glue sneakers to bottom of Styrofoam ball (sketch f).
- Glue eyes onto front of Sports Fan (sketch f).
- Cut a chenille wire in half. Give half to a friend. Cut your piece in half again. Poke one half into each side of Styrofoam ball for arms (sketch f).
- Choose card-stock hands and equipment for your Sports Fan. Cut out and glue onto ends of arms (sketch f).
- To make a pennant, cut out Pennant and Closed Hand patterns. Color pennant. Glue pennant onto toothpick, and then glue toothpick to hand (sketch f).

Simplification Ideas

If children have trouble flattening Styrofoam balls, have them gently rub Styrofoam balls against a concrete walkway. To avoid having children wait for yarn skeins, have some children cut out patterns while others wrap their yarn.

Enrichment Ideas

Children trace card-stock patterns onto craft foam. Provide small doll-sized baseball caps (available at craft stores) for children to glue on top of Pom-Pom Sports Fans. Provide sports ball beads or round wooden beads for children to glue onto Sports Fans' hands or gloves.

a.

b.

c.

d.

e.

knot

f.

Sports Fan Patterns

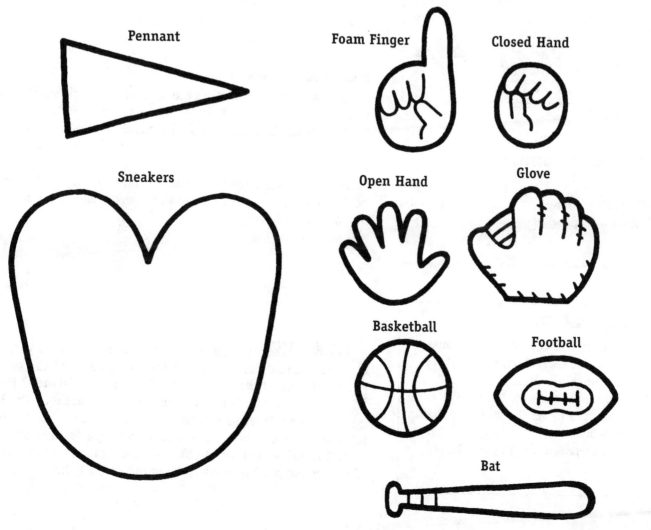

Pennant

Foam Finger

Closed Hand

Sneakers

Open Hand

Glove

Basketball

Football

Bat

Shake It Up! Sports Globe (25-30 MINUTES)

Materials

- ♈ Sports Globe Patterns
- ♈ assorted plastic or metal confetti shapes
- ♈ glitter
- ♈ black permanent fine-tip markers
- ♈ one or more toaster ovens and small cookie sheets
- ♈ oven mitt
- ♈ spoons
- ♈ glycerin (available at pharmacies)
- ♈ dish pan
- ♈ several pitchers of water
- ♈ colored electrical tape

Optional—
- ♈ glue gun

For every three children—
- ♈ one 8x10-inch (20.5x25.5-cm) sheet unprinted shrinkable plastic (available from www.shrinkydinks.com)
- ♈ three 6- to 12-ounce empty glass jars with tight-fitting lids

Standard Supplies

- ♈ scissors
- ♈ shallow containers
- ♈ colored pencils

Preparation

Photocopy one copy of Sports Globe Patterns for each child. Cut plastic sheets in thirds. Pour confetti and glitter into shallow containers. Preheat toaster oven to 325°F. (Optional: Plug in glue gun. Ensure that there is adequate adult supervision for glue gun.)

Instruct each child in the following procedures:

- Choose several designs from the pattern page. Place plastic sheet over desired patterns, and use marker to trace design onto plastic. Or draw your own designs, about the same size as those on the pattern page.
- Use colored pencils to color in designs.
- Cut out plastic designs.
- Place plastic cutouts on cookie sheets.
- With teacher's help, place cookie sheet in oven. Bake pieces until they finish shrinking, about one to three minutes. Remove cookie sheet from toaster oven and allow to cool at least 30 seconds before removing baked cutouts from sheet.
- Place plastic cutouts into jar. Add a spoonful each of confetti and glitter.
- Add a few drops of glycerin to jar.
- Place jar inside dish pan and carefully fill jar to the top with water. Screw lid tightly onto jar. (Optional: With teacher's help, squeeze a line of glue around edge of jar lid to seal.)
- Wrap lid edge with electrical tape to cover.
- Flip jar over and give it a shake!

Simplification Idea

Photocopy patterns directly onto shrinkable plastic sheets. Feed plastic sheets through photocopier, one at a time, using the paper bypass feature. Children color in designs and cut out.

Enrichment Idea

Children decorate a white or orange Ping-Pong ball with permanent markers to look like a baseball or basketball. They place ball in globe before closing.

COACH'S CORNER What do you think would happen if you put your plastic cutouts in the freezer instead of the oven? What if you turned the oven all the way up to broil? Most things work better if you follow the directions. In the Bible, God gives us directions for how to live. God's directions help us know ways to show our love for Him and others. The Bible says, *Strengthen me according to your word. I run in the path of your commands* (Psalm 119:28,32).

tape

Sports Globe Patterns

Torch Pass Game (25-30 MINUTES)

Materials

- ⅞-inch (2.2-cm) dowels
- saw
- metallic spray paint
- red, orange and yellow tissue paper
- gold or silver fabric trim or rickrack

For each child—

- two 2-liter soda bottles
- one 2-inch (5-cm) Styrofoam or foam-rubber ball

Standard Supplies

- scissors
- ruler
- newspaper
- white glue
- shallow containers
- low-temperature glue gun
- large paintbrushes

Preparation

Cut off top half of each soda bottle and discard the bottom. Saw dowels into two 9-inch (23-cm) lengths of for each child. Spray-paint bottles and dowels. Cover work area with newspaper. Pour glue into shallow containers. Plug in glue gun. (Note: Ensure that there is adequate adult supervision for glue gun.)

COACH'S CORNER The world's biggest sporting event, the Olympics, always begins with runners carrying a flame around the world. They pass the flame from one torch to another, all the way from Olympia, Greece, to wherever the Games will take place. The torch run reminds us that people from all countries can compete in the Olympics. When we read the Bible, we learn that people from all countries can be a part of God's team. God loves each person and cares for us. Psalm 100:3 says, *Know that the Lord is God. It is he who made us, and we are his; we are his people.*

Instruct each child in the following procedures:

- Tear tissue paper into flame pieces. Brush glue onto one bottle, covering about 2 inches (5 cm) of the cut edge. Stick tissue flames to bottle, extending past the bottle edge, and then brush glue over tissue (sketch a). Glue a length of trim or rickrack at base of flames (sketch a). Repeat procedure to make a second torch.
- Cover Styrofoam ball with glue and tissue pieces, brushing glue over tissue to smooth it onto the ball (sketch b).
- Use glue gun to glue end of one dowel inside bottle neck to make a torch (sketch c). Repeat procedure with second torch.
- To play Torch Pass: Place flame ball in torch. Hold handle of torch upright and flick wrist to fling ball to a partner. Partner catches ball in torch and flings it back.

Enrichment Idea

Children decorate torches with black permanent markers to give them an embossed look.

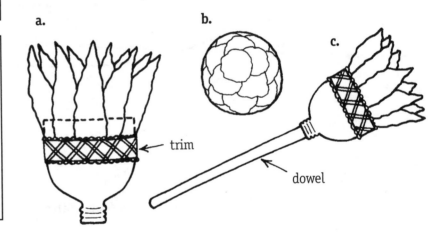

a.

b.

c.

trim

dowel

Get Strong! Barbell

(TWO-DAY CRAFT/35-40 MINUTES TOTAL TIME)

Materials

- ¾-inch (1.9-cm) dowels
- saw
- silver or gray acrylic paint
- glitter-glue pens or paint pens
- plaster of paris
- large mixing bowl
- serving spoons

For each child—
- two empty tuna cans

Standard Supplies

- ruler
- newspaper
- shallow containers
- paintbrushes
- water

COACH'S CORNER

How does a weight lifter get strong? (Lifting weights. Eating healthy foods.) **The members of God's team need to get strong, too, so that they can love and obey God. How can the members of God's team get strong?** (Read and practice what God tells us in His Word, the Bible. Learn about God and worship Him in church and Sunday School.)

DAY ONE Preparation

Saw dowels into one 9-inch (23-cm) length for each child. Cover work area with newspaper. Pour paint into shallow containers.

Instruct each child in the following procedures:

- Paint dowel silver or gray.
- Remove labels from cans. Stand cans on their sides with the open ends facing each other (sketch a). Print the word "Get" on side of left-hand can. Print the word "Strong!" on side of right-hand can.
- With teacher's help, mix plaster according to package directions.
- Spoon wet plaster into one tuna can, filling it almost to the top.
- Stand end of dowel in center of plaster (sketch b).

DAY TWO Preparation

Cover work area with newspaper.

Instruct each child in the following procedures:

- With teacher's help, mix plaster according to package directions.
- Spoon wet plaster into second tuna can, filling it almost to the top.
- Stand free end of dowel in center of plaster (sketch c). Hold or prop in place until plaster sets.

Enrichment Idea

Paint exposed plaster silver or gray.

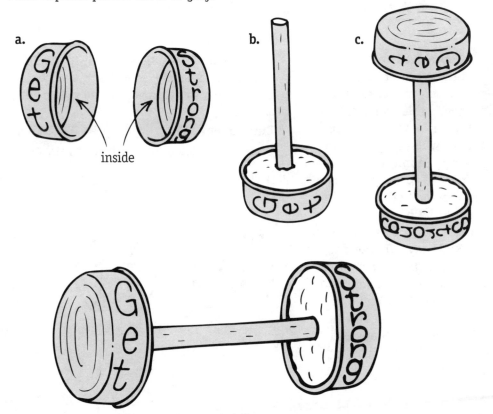

inside

Good Sport's Trinket Box

(TWO-DAY CRAFT/25-30 MINUTES TOTAL TIME)

Materials

- Field and Court Patterns
- acrylic paints in various colors, including green, tan, orange, white and yellow
- white paint pens or correction-fluid pens
- red and black permanent fine-tip markers

For each child—
- 4-inch (10-cm) square papier-mâché box with lid (available at craft stores)
- five ³/₄-inch (1.9-cm) wooden doll-head beads (available at craft stores)

Standard Supplies

- newspaper
- shallow containers
- paintbrushes
- craft glue

COACH'S CORNER What might make a soccer or basketball player feel discouraged? Athletes learn that they have to keep trying, even when they want to give up. People on God's team need to keep loving and obeying God, even when it might be hard. But they never have to do it alone. The Bible says, *Do not fear, for I am with you; do not be dismayed, for I am your God. I will strengthen you and help you* (Isaiah 41:10). **In this verse, what does God promise us?** (He will be with us, strengthen us and help us.)

DAY ONE Preparation

Cover work area with newspaper. Pour paints into shallow containers.

Instruct each child in the following procedures:

- Decide which sport you want to use for your box—soccer, baseball, basketball or tennis.
- Paint outside of box and box lid the color of the playing field or court. Set aside to dry.
- Paint wooden beads an appropriate color for your sport. (Soccer ball—white; basketball—orange; baseball—white; tennis ball—yellow.) Or choose your own colors for sports balls. Set aside to dry.

DAY TWO Preparation

Photocopy one copy of Field and Court Patterns page for each child.

Instruct each child in the following procedures:

- Use white pen or permanent markers to draw field lines on box lid. Use Field and Court Patterns page for examples.
- Use permanent markers to draw details such as stitching and seams on painted beads (sketch a).
- Glue the flat side of one sports ball to the center of the box lid. Glue the remaining four sports balls to the bottom of the box, one in each corner, to serve as feet (sketch b).

Simplification Idea

Omit wooden beads. Glue a small sports-ball shaped eraser onto center of box top for a handle. To make this a one-day craft, spray-paint boxes before class. (Use a spray primer first to save paint.)

Enrichment Idea

Decorate outside of box with sports stickers.

a.

soccer

baseball

basketball

tennis

b.

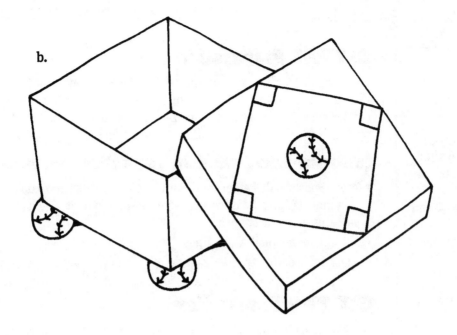

Field and Court Patterns

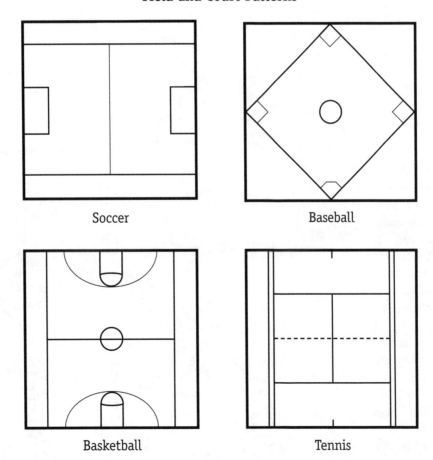

Soccer

Baseball

Basketball

Tennis

Sporty Spiral (TWO-DAY CRAFT/35-40 MINUTES TOTAL TIME)

Materials

- Sports Ball Patterns (p. 85)
- Spiral Pattern
- craft foam in various colors, including white, orange, yellow and brown
- squeeze tubes of T-shirt paint
- colored plastic lacing

For each child—
- one 9x12-inch (23x30.5-cm) sheet of craft foam
- six pony beads

Standard Supplies

- white card stock
- scissors
- pencils
- measuring stick
- hole punches

COACH'S CORNER What do you think it means when people at a sports event say, "It ain't over 'til it's over"? (Don't give up, because it may still be possible to win.) **Even when a sports team starts to get behind, they may still be able to win if they keep trying. Your Sporty Spirals can remind you to keep on loving and obeying God, even when things get tough. God promises to help you at times like that. Isaiah 41:10 says,** *Do not fear, for I am with you; do not be dismayed, for I am your God. I will strengthen you and help you.*

DAY ONE Preparation

Photocopy several copies of Sports Ball Patterns onto card stock. Cut out. Trace the perimeter of Spiral Pattern onto sheets of craft foam to make one for each child. Following the example on the pattern, use a pencil to draw a spiral on each square. Mark holes on each spiral where indicated on pattern.

Instruct each child in the following procedures:

- Trace Sports Ball Patterns of your choice onto craft foam to make five different designs. Or draw your own designs, about the same size as the patterns. Cut out shapes.
- Cut out foam spiral along lines.
- Use T-shirt paints to draw ball details, following examples on patterns.

DAY TWO Preparation

Cut plastic lacing into five 8-inch (20.5-cm) lengths for each child. Cut lacing into one 14-inch (35.5-cm) length for each child.

Instruct each child in the following procedures:

- Use a hole punch to punch holes in spiral where marked and in the top of each foam shape.

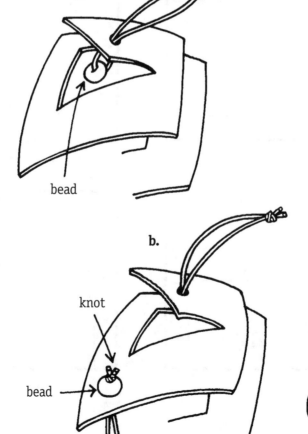

a.

bead

b.

knot

bead

c.

- Thread a pony bead onto the center of the longer length of lacing. From underside of spiral, thread both ends of lacing through hole in spiral center. Tie lacing ends together to make a hanger (sketch a).
- To attach foam shapes to spiral: Thread a foam shape onto the center of a shorter length of lacing. From underside of spiral, thread both ends of lacing through hole in spiral. Thread both ends of lacing through one pony bead. Tie lacing ends together to make a knot (sketch b).

- Attach remaining foam shapes to spiral in the same manner.

Simplification Idea

Cut out plain circles and football shapes from various colors of foam before class. Students decorate with permanent markers to look like sports balls.

Spiral Pattern

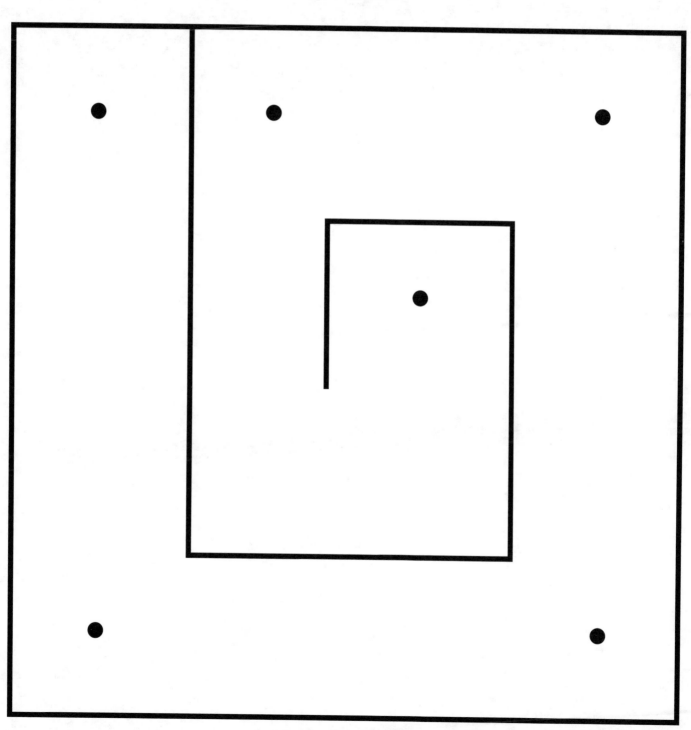

Section Four

Bonus Pages

Terry

KEPT ON
and memorized all the
Bible Memory Verses at

SonGames

2004

WAY 2 GO

Team Visors

Use these ideas for decorating foam visors for each class at your Vacation Bible School, church camp or school.

Sports Ball Patterns

Use these simple patterns for several crafts in this book. Or photocopy and enlarge them onto appropriate colors of construction paper and cut out for an easy room decoration.

Artist Labels

Use these patterns to make labels to identify the owner of each craft. Each label includes an age-appropriate Bible memory verse.

Certificates and Awards

The awards and certificates on the following pages may be personalized for various uses. Just follow these simple steps:

1. Tear out certificate, and print the name of your program on the appropriate line.

2. Photocopy as many copies of certificate as needed.

3. Print each child's certificate with his or her name (and achievement when appropriate).

Sticker Poster

1. Photocopy a sticker poster for each student.

2. After students color posters, attach posters to a wall or bulletin board.

3. Have students add stickers to their posters each day as they arrive. Or use stickers as rewards for reciting Bible memory verses, being helpful or completing assignments.

Coloring Pages

Prekindergarten and Kindergarten Coloring Pages

These large simple pictures are designed for the littlest artists in your program. Each page also contains a simple Bible verse.

Bible Memory Verse Coloring Pages

Use these fun-to-color designs to reinforce Bible memory verses. There are five pages for younger elementary children and five for older elementary children.

SonGames Motto Coloring Pages

These bold designs will help kids remember five aspects of being on God's team.

Use these reproducible coloring pages in any of the following ways:

• Use as awards for children who memorize the Bible verse. They may take them home to color and display.

• Photocopy a set of coloring pages for each student. Cover with a folded sheet of construction paper and staple to make a coloring book.

• Use in class for transition times or for students who finish an activity ahead of other students.

• Play a coloring game. Place a variety of markers on the table. Recite the verse together. Then each student may choose a marker and use it to color on his or her design for one minute. When time is up, students put markers down and repeat verse together again. Students then choose another marker and color for one minute. Repeat process until coloring is completed or students tire of activity.

• Customize any coloring page by covering the Bible verse with white paper and printing another verse or saying in its place before you photocopy.

Team Visors

Use a different color of visor to distinguish each class at your Vacation Bible School, camp or school. Precut craft-foam visors are available from Gospel Light. Or make your own, following the "Optional" instructions from the Pennant Visor craft (p. 24).

Let each child personalize his or her visor. Provide a variety of decorative materials, along with scissors and glue. Then stand back and see what develops!

Glue-Ons and Stick-Ons
- craft-foam cutouts
- paper die-cuts
- stickers
- wiggle eyes
- acrylic gems
- sequins
- beads
- buttons
- pom-poms
- rickrack
- chenille wire
- silk flowers
- tissue paper

Draw-Ons and Paint-Ons
- gel pens
- glitter glue
- paint pens
- permanent markers
- T-shirt paints
- acrylic paints

Stick-Ups and Dangle-Offs
- pom-pom trim
- discarded earrings
- toothpick flags
- feathers

84

Sports Ball Patterns

Artist Labels

Use these labels to identify crafts. Photocopy page and cut apart on the bold lines.
Children write their names on labels and glue to crafts.

Early Childhood	Younger Elementary	Older Elementary
Handmade by "God made us and we are his." (See Psalm 100:3.)	Handmade by "Know that the Lord is God. It is he who made us, and we are his." Psalm 100:3	Handmade by "Know that the Lord is God. It is he who made us, and we are his; we are his people." Psalm 100:3
Handmade by "Help each other show love." (See Hebrews 10:24.)	Handmade by "Let us consider how we may spur one another on toward love and good deeds." Hebrews 10:24	Handmade by "Let us consider how we may spur one another on toward love and good deeds." Hebrews 10:24
Handmade by "I am quick to obey God's Word." (See Psalm 119:32.)	Handmade by "Strengthen me according to your word." Psalm 119:28	Handmade by "Strengthen me according to your word. I run in the path of your commands." Psalm 119:28,32
Handmade by "Do not fear, for I am with you." Isaiah 41:10	Handmade by "Do not fear, for I am with you. . . . I will strengthen you and help you." Isaiah 41:10	Handmade by "Do not fear, for I am with you; do not be dismayed, for I am your God. I will strengthen you and help you." Isaiah 41:10
Handmade by "Thanks be to God!" 1 Corinthians 15:57	Handmade by "Thanks be to God! He gives us the victory through our Lord Jesus Christ." 1 Corinthians 15:57	Handmade by "Thanks be to God! He gives us the victory through our Lord Jesus Christ." 1 Corinthians 15:57

"God made us and we are his."

(See Psalm 100:3.)

"Help each other show love."
(See Hebrews 10:24.)

"I am quick to obey God's Word." (See Psalm 119:32.)

Prekindergarten/Kindergarten Coloring Page 3

"Do not fear, for I am with you."

Isaiah 41:10

"Thanks be to God!"

1 Corinthians 15:57

"Know that the Lord is God. It is he who made us, and we are his." Psalm 100:3

"Let us consider how we may spur one another on toward love and good deeds."

Hebrews 10:24

"Strengthen me according to your word." Psalm 119:28

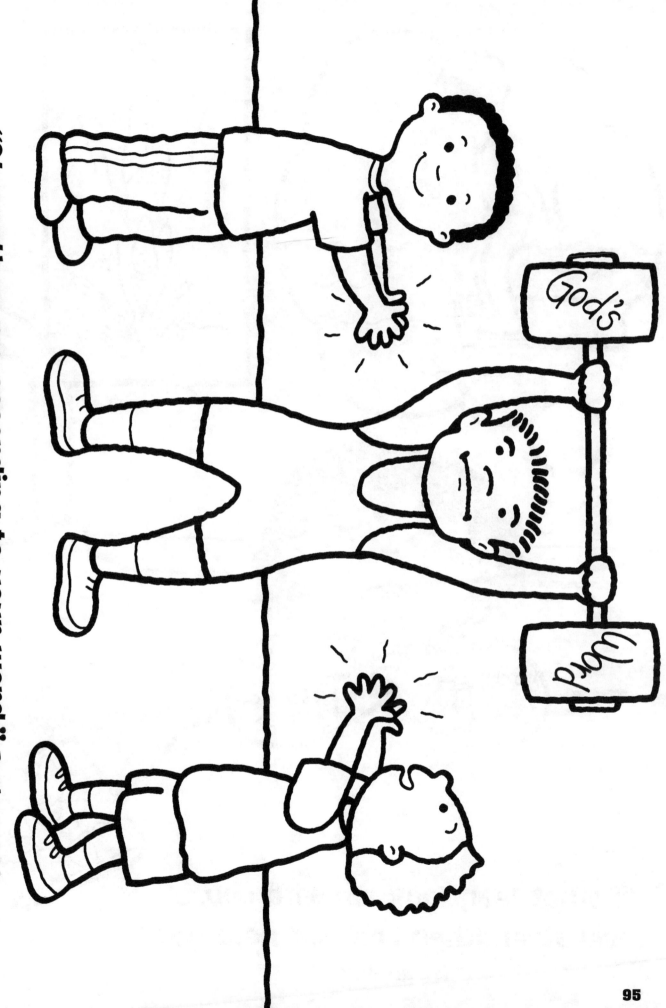

"Do not fear, for I am with you. . . .
I will strengthen you and help you."
Isaiah 41:10

"Thanks be to God! He gives us the victory through our Lord Jesus Christ." 1 Corinthians 15:57

Know that the
Lord is God.

It is he who made
us, and we are his;

We are
his people.
Psalm 100:3

"Let us consider how we may spur one another on toward love and good deeds."

Hebrews 10:24

"Strengthen me according to your word. I run in the path of your commands."

Psalm 119:28,32

do not be dismayed, for I am your God.

Do not fear, for I am with you;

I WILL STRENGTHEN YOU AND HELP YOU.

Isaiah 41:10

Thanks be to God! He gives us the Victory through our Lord Jesus Christ. 1 Corinthians 15:57

GOOD SPORT AWARD

_____

WAS A GREAT TEAM MEMBER AT

_____.

VISITOR AWARD

_____

WE'RE GLAD YOU JOINED IN AT

_____.

made a splash by

at

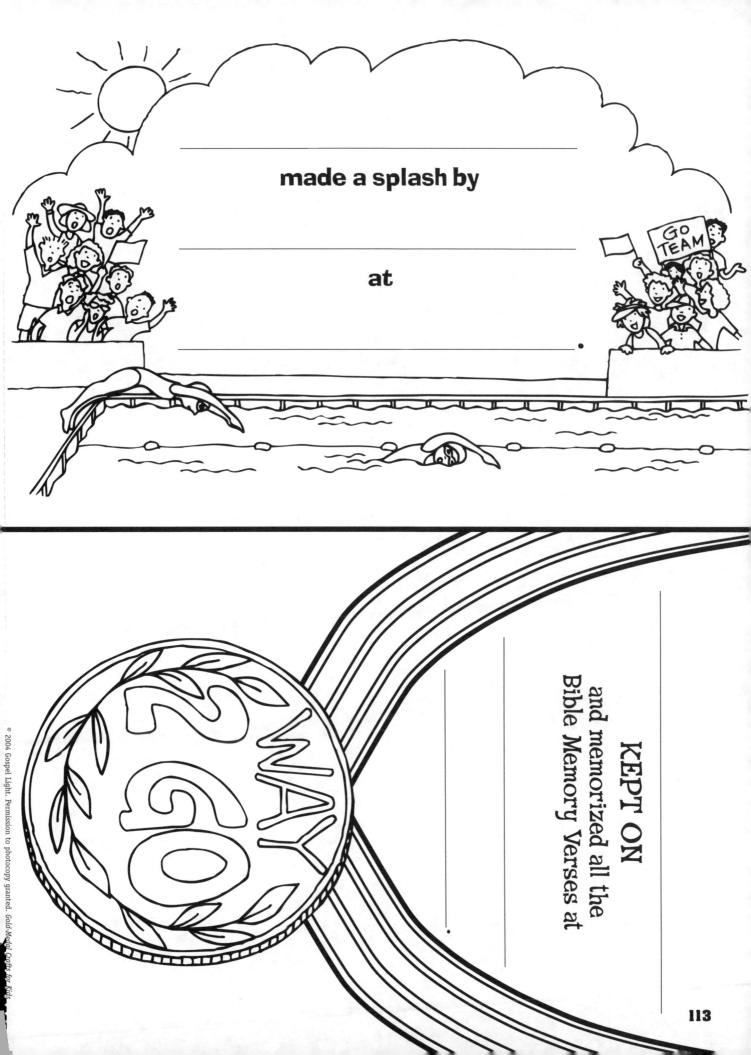

WAY 2 GO

KEPT ON
and memorized all the
Bible *Memory Verses* at

Thanks for carrying the torch at

_____.

THANKS,

_____,

for

_____

at

_____.

Grazie

Arigato

Danke Schön

Spasibo

Tack

Gracias

Celebrate

Attendance Award

presented to

for attendance at

117

Sticker Poster

Index of Crafts

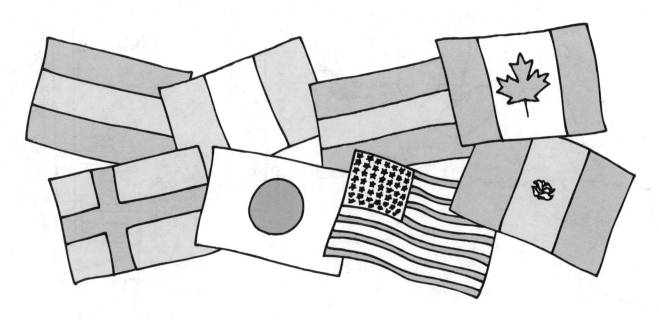